P9-CDB-556

Green
ARCHITECTURE

ABOVE
Low Energy Houses,
Hjortekaer, Denmark

FOLLOWING PAGES
Insulated walls of Glenn
Murcutt's Kempsey Museum,
New South Wales
Façade of apartments, Les
Garennes, Saint-Quentin-en-
Yvelines, near Paris, with
individual sunspaces

BRENDA AND ROBERT VALE

Green
ARCHITECTURE
Design for an energy-conscious future

A BULFINCH PRESS BOOK
LITTLE, BROWN AND COMPANY
Boston · Toronto · London

Copyright © 1991 by Thames and Hudson Ltd, London

All rights reserved. No part of this book may be reproduced in any
form or by any elctronic or mechanical means, including information storage
and retrieval systems, without permission in writing from the publisher,
except by a reviewer who may quote brief passages in a review.

First United States Edition

Library of Congress Cataloging-in-Publication Data

Vale, Brenda
        Green Architecture : design for an energy–conscious future / Brenda and
    Robert Vale. — 1st U.S. ed.
        p. cm.
        Includes bibliographical refernces and index.
        ISBN 0-8212-1866-2
        1. Architecture and energy conservation.   I. Vale, Robert James
    Dennis.   II. Title.
    NA2542.3.v35   1991
    720'.472—dc20
                                                                            91-8656

Bulfinch Press is an imprint and trademark of Little, Brown and Company (Inc.)
Published simultaneously in Canada by Little, Brown & Company (Canada) Limited

PRINTED IN SINGAPORE

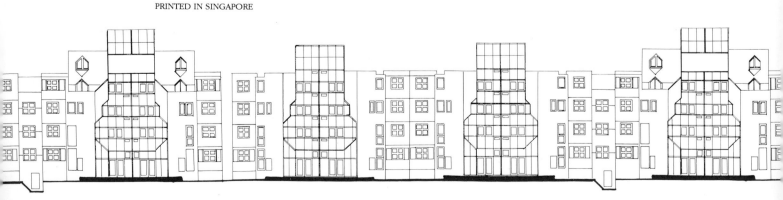

CONTENTS

INTRODUCTION

Attitudes to architecture

Listen to Le Corbusier in 1927:
You employ stone, wood and concrete, and with these
materials you build houses and palaces; that is construction.
Ingenuity is at work.
But suddenly you touch my heart,
you do me good, I am happy and I say: 'This is beautiful'.
That is architecture. Art enters in.[1]

VERY few would dare to question the validity of this statement. It is accepted that architecture has a quality which allows it to rise above ordinary building and that there exists a recognizable difference between the two. Much argument can then be brought forward in an effort to establish the agreed dividing line. The missing person in the debate, however, is usually the consumer of architecture. It is up to the consumer to be moved by the architecture; and if the consumer is not moved by the building, then it is the consumer who has not been educated, or who has failed to understand the purpose of the architect. As architecture itself becomes increasingly specialized and divided, so the common base from which designer and consumer start becomes eroded.

A 'green' dimension to such issues recognizes that a common base must exist between all concerned, whether artist or lay person. Since the journey into space, the fragility of the world has both shocked and challenged. It has become apparent how dependent each person is on the next, for all belong to the same whole. The single shared experience is that of living on the same, very small, Earth. The way in which one person makes an alteration to the planet must have an effect on the other 4,999,999,999 inhabitants.

If it is possible to recognize the interde-

pendence of all, so at the same time the gulf between the expert and the lay consumer of buildings seems ever widening. In the days of vernacular architecture, the consumers of building understood the process of construction, even if they were not themselves builders. This is no longer true. Some would argue that the vernacular tradition was never architecture, only building, and that unless aesthetics predominate, 'architecture' does not exist. In his writing on the subject Brunskill describes the architectural process as follows:

> Aesthetically and, probably, constructionally the designer will have been adventurous, exploring new ways of achieving his conscious wishes; in so doing his materials will have been chosen to help achieve the aesthetic or constructional end and have been obtained from whatever source could supply such materials.[2]

Here, Brunskill is suggesting that 'true' architecture will override considerations of the ready availability of resources in pursuit of an aesthetic effect, whereas the vernacular tradition relied upon the best *use* of the available resources, with traditional building methods guiding what was done in any par-

Interior of King House, Santa Fe, New Mexico, built of timber and earth, with a heavy mass structure to store the sun's warmth

ticular place. Aesthetic considerations were nonetheless part of the design, hence the delight in symmetry and order that appears in vernacular building.

However, the failure to link 'true' architecture with a concern for resources dates back at least to the origins of the classical tradition, a tradition that some would still regard as a relevant architectural concern of today. In his discussion of Greek architecture, J. J. Coulton suggests that a monumental architecture, that is, 'buildings intended to impress and endure, not just perform a function',[3] only made its appearance in the Greek world in the seventh century B C. From the start this architecture was an exploration and perfection of a structurally unsophisticated system.

> The basic system remained a post-and-lintel structure executed in large, carefully dressed stone blocks. This structural conservatism is probably inherent in the Greek conception of architecture as concerned primarily with external form rather than internal space.[4]

Monumental architecture, from its beginnings, is associated with a profligate attitude to resources. This, in turn, suggests that architecture is only to be available for those who have the wealth to hold this attitude towards resources. From this early time dates not only the divorce of architecture from the common and the ordinary, but also an association of architecture with the economic surplus necessary for the production of art. Even without the class structure of ancient Greek society that distinguished between the wealth-holders and the wealth-creators, architecture had no connection with the lowest in society, who would understand the simple struggle to produce the best possible shelter for the least expenditure of resources, be the resources material or labour. Architecture became associated, not with the production of shelter, but with the expenditure of resources for a particular stylistic effect.

Although the Greeks understood the principle of the arch, they did not use it in their architecture except in cellars and underground vaults, even though the technology of

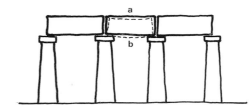

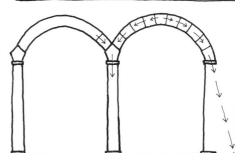

A simple stone lintel (top) bends under load. Surface **a** is in compression, **b** in tension. Stone is weak and breaks easily in tension, so the lintel is deep and the span limited. An arch (below) carries only compressive loads. The thrust is carried from block to block and so to the ground. Less stone is required to span a given width, and columns can be wider apart

its construction used less stone to create any given size of enclosure. It is tempting to suggest that the exploitation of the arch in the later Roman architecture was a way of coping with the shortfall of resources for a more concentrated population. Medieval architects showed further how the arch form could minimize the use of resources by covering the maximum space with the smallest quantity of material; the development of Gothic architecture between the Romanesque and the Perpendicular in England illustrates this trend. Although the buildings that remain to us from this period are the great public monuments, as with Greece, here there may be more relationship between the ordinary building for shelter and the monumental architecture of the church, as both are grounded in the best use of the available resources. Whereas the monumental architecture of Greece must be associated with a society that relied on slavery, the monumental architecture of the medieval period was produced during a time when slavery was eliminated and the common people, as part of a complex hierarchy, were recognized as more than just a resource to be exploited.

Such arguments are of necessity provocative generalizations; but at the present time the call for a return to classicism has to be set against an increasing realization that the

The Romanesque portions of Peterborough Cathedral, nave, transepts and choir (below), have a massive stone structure and small windows. The much later retro-choir in the Perpendicular style (top) has a greatly increased area of glazing to stone. Less material is used to enclose the same volume

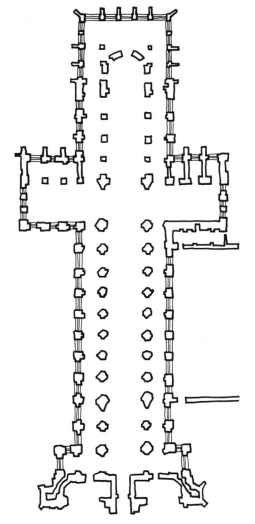

resources of this planet are not infinite. It has been written that:

> Many people think that a revival of classicism can help. It is certainly a universal language but it is not one that can be applied easily unless it is thoroughly learned.[5]

In reply, it might be said that classicism is not supposed to be a common architectural language (not, perhaps, the language of the street), but is best suited to the public building and the monumental face of the built environment. However, what this advocacy implies is that where architecture matters most, in the 'grand' buildings that reflect the way society views itself, resources are unimportant; that while it may be suitable to build low-energy houses and small buildings that demonstrate the use of natural materials, it is not appropriate for such architectural concerns to figure in, for example, the design of new buildings around St Paul's Cathedral in London. Until a great resource-conscious public building has been commissioned by private or government agencies, no amount of 'green' talk by politicians will count for anything in the built environment. In some countries these issues have been recognized as important, but the current issues of Western architecture suggest that life is to impinge less and less on the art of building.

It is almost as if architecture has to deny its link with 'real' building in order to sustain artistic credibility. As an instance, the two differing attitudes towards the essence of shelter, embodied in the primitive hut, of the Abbé Laugier and Henry Thoreau can be compared.

When the Abbé Laugier contemplated the simplicity of the primitive hut as a basis for architecture, his analysis, although it recognized that man in the forest had to put together the branches to make the hut, was entirely visual:

> Let us never lose sight of our little rustic hut. I can only see columns, a ceiling or entablature and a pointed roof forming at both ends what is called a pediment . . . I

therefore come to this conclusion: in an architectural Order only the column, the entablature and the pediment may form an essential part of its composition. If each of these parts is suitably placed and suitably formed, nothing else need be added to make the work perfect.[6]

The engraving that fronted the Abbé Laugier's *Essai sur l'architecture* (1753) shows no builder of the primitive hut but rather a figure representing the designer, with compasses in hand, who is to transpose the visual characteristics of the primitive wooden shelter into stone, and subsequently the classical tradition. With this transposition the divorce of the building from the user is begun, for the properties of stone are very different from the properties of wood. Referring back to the writings of Vitruvius, who supposed that the classical tradition in some way represented a translation of the rudiments of a timber architecture into stone, Laugier proposes a

TOP AND RIGHT
The classical tradition of the Parthenon (top) is re-interpreted to clothe conventional office blocks in a plan for office re-development near St Paul's Cathedral, London. Architect: John Simpson

simplification of architecture back to the fundamental parts of shelter: column, beam and roof. Historically, following his writings, the decorative whimsy of the Rococo was dismissed in favour of the classical severity of Neoclassicism. At no point, however, did Laugier consider that architecture should be concerned with the best use of resources. The classical tradition, although claiming to respect nature, has failed to realize its dependence upon it.

Thus, although the classical tradition relies on a contrast between what nature is and what man can make, its aim is to find the point of balance between the two to create harmony. What it ignores is the fundamental relationship between the works of man and the raw materials of nature. As the picture on the following page shows, the classical pavilion is set isolated, yet positioned so that the composition is dependent upon the existence of both landscape and building. It is reliant upon nature but apart, an architecture of both

Geoffrey Bawa's Parliament Building, Sri Lanka, uses traditional forms and local materials, and relies on natural ventilation and shading for comfortable conditions inside the building

The designer fronting the Abbé Laugier's *Essai sur l'Architecture* of 1753 is about to transpose the forms suggested by a simple rustic shelter into the very different medium of stone, and into the classical tradition of architecture. Here style takes precedence over considerations of purpose and the nature of materials

leisure and plentiful resources. It turns its back upon nature, but must use the resources of nature to create the artifice.

In contrast, the view of the primitive hut that Thoreau gives is one of human life as part of nature rather than in opposition to it. The human intelligence is never separated from the recognition of natural laws:

> It is well to have some water in your neighbourhood, to give buoyancy and to float the earth. One value even of the smallest well is, that when you look into it you see that earth is not continent but insular. This is as important as that it keeps the butter cool.[7]

It is important that Thoreau should accept both ideas in the same moment: the natural properties of the well that man may use without destroying them, and the reminder of the system within which man must exist.

The place of architecture within the system is also made clear. As Brecht said: '*Erst kommt das Fressen, dann kommt die Moral*';[8] or, as Thoreau stated more explicitly: 'they can do without architecture who have no olives nor wines in the cellar'.[9] Thoreau's recognition of the subservience of art to the equitable access to resources, so that all may be adequately fed and sheltered, must underlie any green approach to architecture.

As for the hut itself, it is the process of construction and the performance of the finished work that interests Thoreau in his description of the building of his own simple shelter at Walden. The primitive hut is examined, not from the viewpoint of its external appearance, but from the amount of wood and other materials that were necessary to construct the shelter, the cost of the same both in terms of money and of labour to cut and move, and how comfortable the house is to live in and how easy to keep clean. The only description of the appearance of the hut is brief:

> I have thus a tight shingled and plastered house, ten feet wide by fifteen long, and eight-feet posts, with a garret and a closet, a large window on each side, two trap doors, one door at the end, and a brick fireplace opposite.[10]

Furthermore, although Thoreau agrees with the importance of the humble dwelling as a subject for the painter, it is the lives of those who live within the dwelling that make it a suitable subject for study, not the symbolic quality of the method of construction: 'It is the life of the inhabitants whose shells they are, and not any peculiarity in their surfaces merely, which makes them picturesque....'[11] Architecture is recognized by Thoreau for what it is, a container that is to be subservient to the lives of those whom it affects; whereas the definition offered by Laugier divorces architecture from those whom it affects through the use of symbolic images offered to those educated to understand them:

> The entablature is the second part which appears in the model of the rustic hut.

The pieces of wood which rest horizontally on the vertical posts to form a ceiling are represented by what we call the entablature.[12]

The model of architecture offered by Thoreau places far more responsibility on the designer than the model offered by Laugier. If architecture is to be subservient, then it must take account, not just of the way the building satisfies the immediate users, or even of the way in which it becomes part of the public realm, but of every person remotely affected by it. If this necessitates designing buildings that will not help to trigger a chain of global climatic events that may lead to the flooding of low-lying areas of the world, then this concern, too, must become the responsibility of the designer.

An architecture so broadly subservient to the needs of people will be an architecture that is more, not less, difficult to achieve. Proportion and symbolism are more limited concerns than the technical response required for a building to 'touch-this-earth-lightly'.[13] To follow the model for the primitive hut argued by Thoreau is to return to simplicity of design on a basis that is far

more complex. It becomes necessary to consider the 'web'[14] of which the building forms a part, and the effect of the insertion of a new structure into this web.

Every inhabitant of the planet has some understanding of the weather that results from the effect of climate on local terrain. Even those sufficiently wealthy to spend their time within air-conditioned buildings, transported between them in air-conditioned vehicles, cannot fail to observe if not experience weather. The language of modification of climate is the common language of architecture, enriched by the vast range of responses necessary to meet all global conditions. This was recognized by Thoreau in his exposition on the primitive hut:

> I took particular pleasure in this breaking of ground, for in almost all latitudes men dig into the earth for an equable temperature.[15]

Thoreau here recognizes a common problem and a solution, and gains pleasure from the repetition of a task executed by many at different times and in different places. Even in a wealthy society where the built environ-

The classical building of Claude's painting of the *Rest on the Flight into Egypt* has no function. Its only purpose is to balance the composition and point the contrast between the man-made and the natural

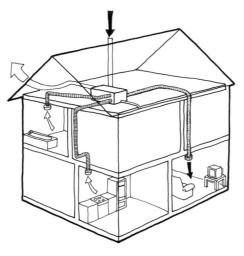

A simple 'Do-it-yourself' heat recovery system, allowing the user access to up-to-date technology. Warmth otherwise lost from the kitchen and bathroom is used to pre-heat the fresh air supply to the living rooms

ment is mainly in the hands of experts, the wish to continue with the traditional common task can be recognized in the success of the 'Do-it-yourself' industry. It may be no accident that the level of resource-conserving technology available to the public through Do-it-yourself stores is sometimes in advance of that generally available in the housing market.

It is not necessary to be an expert to know the common language. Whether one is trying to keep the sun out or welcome it into a building, solutions to the specific problem will depend upon a common appreciation of the character and action of sunlight. What Thoreau presents and Laugier obscures is a built form that is meaningful to the many because all understand its basic premise.

To continue to build an architecture based on another premise is to invite future censure. What is required is for designers once again to realize a shared experience with users of buildings, and a shared responsibility for the Earth's resources.

As car design has moved from a concern with surface styling to a concentrated effort to improve engineering performance, so architecture needs to be similarly distanced from its current concern for appearance only. It is time to stop putting the fins on the Cadillac.

1 PURPOSE

Architecture and the survival of the planet

To the ancients, all matter was composed of the four elements of earth, water, fire and air, in varying proportions. Today the composition of matter is known to be far more complex, but the four elements still provide a useful way of looking at how buildings interact with the world. For buildings are constructed of materials taken from the earth, they are serviced with water and 'fire', and they interact with the air, water, 'fire' and earth that their occupants depend upon for survival.

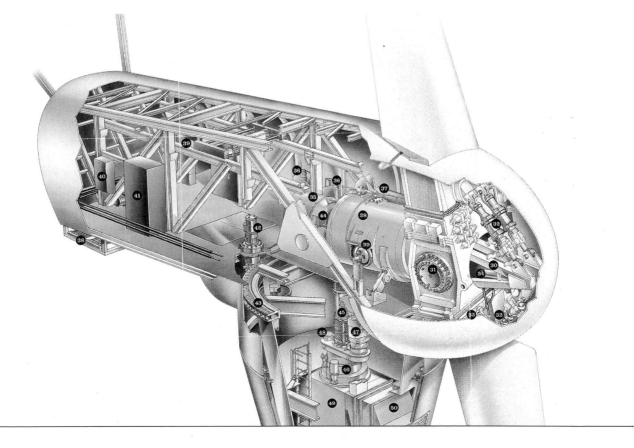

An early Ford production line, innocent first steps in a process whose end cannot be foreseen

ONE purpose of Thoreau's sojourn by Walden Pond was to show that a man can live without becoming alienated from the natural world. The ideas of harmony rather than opposition to nature, of technology which is immediately needful rather than developed for its own sake, are not new. Some would claim that the whole history of science and technology has been beset by those of a Luddite[1] tendency who question the need for further exploration and experiment. The 'Luddites' in their turn point to the seemingly pointless developments in technology and question the need for resources to be used in this way. The debate caused by this dilemma has often blocked a possible third path for science and technology; that is, the development of needful and sustainable technologies that make the best use of resources, a development that has variously been termed alternative or appropriate technology.

The approach of appropriate technology can be illustrated by a Hindu story:

A king of ancient India, oppressed by the roughness of the earth upon soft human feet, proposed that his whole territory should be carpeted with skins. However, one of his wise men pointed out that the same result could be achieved far more simply by taking a single skin and cutting

off small pieces to bind beneath the feet. These were the first sandals.[2]

The appropriate technology produces a solution that makes the best use of the available resources and has minimum effect on the *status quo*. Such an approach is not limited to Eastern societies but can be found traditionally in the West enshrined in such wisdoms as 'horses for courses'. The complexity of modern science where, like the designer, the scientist is an expert divorced from the needs of the public has concentrated interest in a limited field of development and encouraged participants to narrow their terms of reference. Education encourages specialization, and the generalist courses where two or more disciplines are combined are considered to be second best and for the weaker students. Such compartmentalized approach can encourage the development of a seemingly absurd level of technology.

It is possible to see a similar division in the field of design. The discipline of architecture was originally one that allowed the arts and technology to meet and to be subsumed into the synthesis of building. It is reasonable to suggest that it was the proliferation of technologies that came with industrialization that began the split between the artist-designer and the technologist-engineer:

At the outset ... the elementary uses of iron were easy for an architect to understand; or, if in doubt, a 'practical man' could be called on for assistance. But at its maturity a generation or so later, the understanding of iron had slipped beyond the grasp of most architects, who relinquished the territory to engineers and ironwork contractors.[3]

LEFT AND CENTRE
The ancient monuments of Athens (left) have received more damage from pollution over the last twenty-five years than over the past twenty-four centuries. The acid rain that dissolves building materials and the Los Angeles-type of air pollution are just two of the problems that can only be solved by the application of green technologies and principles of design

However, the split can also be linked to the economic realities of industrialization, where the speed of construction was often more important than the quality of the finished product, and speed required division and specialization of tasks within an overall framework. Speed became the goal, and with it came the impossibility of one mind overseeing the whole task. It is therefore not surprising that the implications of what was produced became hidden by the disaggregation of the tasks, and technology could develop without anybody pointing out the imbalance between the technology and the natural world.

At a time, far distant, when all matter living and inanimate was thought to be composed of the four elements of earth, water, fire, air,[4] the nature of matter, its properties and behaviour, could be understood in relation to these naturally occurring phenomena. Scientific understanding was formed directly from an observation of nature. The splintering and complexity of modern science has contributed to a world view wherein even an object as simple as a building is described in terms of its component parts – wall, roof, boiler, drain – with no language of description to describe the interaction of the parts to achieve the whole. Only recently have such phrases as 'the function of the roof', 'the function of the wall', been replaced by a far more holistic notion, 'the behaviour of the building envelope'.

It is tempting to borrow the ancient view, and imagine the built environment as poised between the four ancient elements – earth, water, air, fire – and interacting with each. At present such interaction is largely destructive rather than sympathetic. However, if the interactions were to become the focus, rather than the building or built environment, then it might be possible to reinstate these relationships around a sustainable and appropriate level of technology.

Air

The destruction of Earth's atmosphere

Forget six counties overhung
with smoke,
Forget the snorting steam and
piston stroke,
Forget the spreading of the
hideous town ...[5]

Environmental pollution is not a new concern. When William Morris began his epic poetic work 'The Earthly Paradise' with these words in 1868, he was reacting against the

'London going out of Town – or – the march of bricks and mortar'. Rapid urbanization as seen by the cartoonist George Cruickshank in 1835

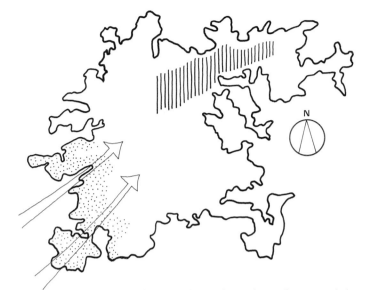

||||| Industrial zone

⠿ Zone of most
desirable housing

Housing of the well-to-do in
Sheffield, England, protected
from pollution by the
prevailing wind

effects of the Industrial Revolution and the unbridled urban growth of nineteenth-century England. His hatred for both the environmental damage he saw around him and the society that produced it were not widely shared by his contemporaries, who tended to see pollution as an unfortunate but inescapable side effect of wealth creation. Their response was to try to avoid the worst of it, as can be seen in cities like Sheffield, where the houses of the rich tend to be grouped to the south west, comfortably upwind of the smoking industries that produced their wealth.

Following the United Nations conference on the environment in Stockholm in 1972, there was a brief upsurge of interest in environmental matters such as pollution and resource depletion. The idea that oil might not last for ever was given further popular emphasis as a result of the OPEC oil embargo in the mid-1970s, when motorists suddenly could not obtain all the fuel they wanted.

In 1920 Thomas Midgley, a research scientist working for General Motors, discovered a cheap chemical that could be added to relatively low-grade petrol to improve its octane rating and prevent engine knocking. It was a breakthrough in improving the efficiency of the petrol engine.[6] In 1930 Midgley, now working for the Frigidaire Division of General Motors, was asked by his employers to produce an alternative for the unsafe am-

monia that was then in use as a refrigerant. In two days he came up with a group of cheap, stable, non-toxic and non-flammable chemicals that would do the job. He demonstrated the characteristics of his invention by taking a mouthful of the new chemical and then blowing out a candle flame. Mdigley's chemicals found widespread application in refrigeration, aerosols, fire extinguishers, and the manufacture of the insulation foams used in buildings.[7]

Thomas Midgley's 1920 invention was leaded petrol; his 1930 success was chlorofluorocarbons (CFCs).

In the 1970s, following the increased environmental awareness fostered by the Stockholm conference, some scientists suggested that CFCs used as propellants in aerosols could damage the Earth's stratospheric ozone layer. A report published by the UK Department of the Environment in 1976 said that 'scientifically the hypotheses put forward are plausible and therefore warrant serious attention', and concluded, 'attempts should be made to seek alternatives'.[8] This recommendation was based on research which

The architect as land-hungry monster, T-square in one hand and copy of planning consent in the other, a drawing by the American architect Malcolm Wells

showed that at 1973 rates of usage of CFCs, 'a maximum depletion of about 8 per cent in the ozone layer will occur in about one hundred years' time'. The report also looked at the link between CFCs and global warming, and stated 'calculations indicate ... the surface temperature will rise by about 1 degree K'. The use of these chemicals in aerosol sprays was banned in the USA and Scandinavia because it was relatively easy to find alternative propellant gases. The manufacturers of CFCs claimed that the evidence for their damaging effects was inconclusive, and continued to make them. However, in 1985 measurements reported in a paper in the scientific journal *Nature*[9] showed that a hole was appearing in the ozone layer above Antarctica. This was totally unexpected, since it had not been predicted by the current computer models of ozone creation and destruction in the atmosphere. Further international research proved the link between CFCs and the ozone hole.[10]

The significance of the ozone layer in the stratosphere (the upper atmosphere) is that it protects the Earth and its occupants from damaging ultra-violet radiation. Ozone is formed in the stratosphere by the action of sunlight on oxygen atoms. Until the formation of the ozone layer billions of years ago, complex forms of life could not develop on the planet. If the ozone layer is destroyed, the future of life on Earth is uncertain. Even a 1 per cent decrease in stratospheric ozone suggests an 8 per cent increase in human skin

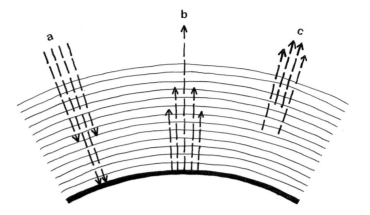

cancers due to increased ultra-violet exposure. Ultra-violet radiation is also linked to the formation of cataracts, and to diseases which enter the body through the skin such as bilharzia and herpes. Many food crops are adversely affected by increased ultra-violet exposure, as are phytoplankton, the tiny ocean plants which form the base of the ocean food chain.[11] Phytoplankton are also part of the mechanism by which carbon dioxide is taken out of the atmosphere.

CFCs are very stable in the atmosphere, and will continue to migrate slowly upwards to do their damage even after their use has been discontinued. The Montreal Protocol of 1 January 1989, an international agreement which seeks to commit the industrialized nations to a halving of CFC consumption by the end of the century, will result in a threefold increase in stratospheric ozone early in the next century. Each atom of chlorine from a CFC molecule can help destroy 100,000 ozone molecules in the stratosphere.

The destruction of the ozone layer is only one of the large-scale climatic experiments that human beings are conducting. Human activities are altering the composition of the atmosphere in such a way that it traps more of the sun's heat. This is the so-called 'greenhouse effect'. The temperature inside a greenhouse rises when the sun shines on it because the glass is relatively transparent to the short-wave solar radiation and allows it to enter easily. When the radiation strikes the earth and plants in the greenhouse they are heated and give off long-wave heat radiation.

The 'greenhouse effect'.
a Solar radiation, reaching the Earth and warming it.
b Radiation from Earth's surface, partly absorbed by carbon dioxide and water vapour in the atmosphere.
c Radiant heat lost from the atmosphere to space.
If a, b and c are not in balance, the temperature of the atmosphere will rise

RIGHT
The global temperature trend. The dotted line shows annual mean temperatures, the solid line the five-year running mean (after F. Pearce, *Turning up the Heat*, 1989)

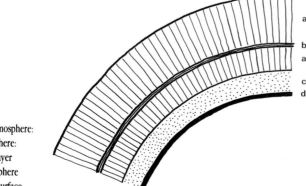

Earth's atmosphere:
a stratosphere:
b ozone layer
c trophosphere
d Earth's surface

This is less able to pass through the glass, which is relatively opaque to radiation at these longer wavelengths.

Certain gases in the atmosphere act like the glass in a greenhouse. They allow solar radiation to enter and warm the surface of the Earth, but they prevent the longer-wave heat radiation from escaping back into space. The Earth maintains a thermal equilibrium because the energy coming in from the sun is balanced by the heat that flows out. If less heat flows out because it is trapped in the atmosphere, the Earth's temperature will rise.

The principal 'greenhouse gas' is carbon dioxide (CO_2), which contributes about half of the total global warming effect. About 80 per cent of the carbon dioxide comes from the burning of fossil fuels (coal, oil and gas), the remaining 20 per cent from the burning of forests and firewood, and from agricultural sources.[12]. The atmosphere at present contains more than 700 billion tonnes of carbon and fossil fuels are adding about 6 billion tonnes per year. However, the known fossil fuel reserves of the Earth represent a total of 7,500 billion tonnes of carbon, most of which would be added to the atmosphere if all the fuels were burned (some would be taken up by the oceans).

A further 18 per cent of global warming comes from the gas methane (CH_4). This is produced by bacteria that break down organic matter in the absence of oxygen in places such as swamps and bogs; the marsh gas that is occasionally seen burning on the surface of such places is largely methane. Methane is also produced in refuse tips, where garbage decomposes to form the gas. It is sometimes burned off because it is explosive when mixed with air and hazardous to local residents. A major source of methane is the stomachs of ruminants such as cows and sheep. The increasing demand for meat and dairy produce has led to a doubling of the world's cow population between 1960 and 1980. A single cow emits about 200 litres of methane per day. The calorific value of this quantity of gas is about 1.5 kWh which means that the eructations of a herd of thirty cows would be enough to provide the central heating and hot water for a three-bedroom semi-detached house, provided that the gas could be collected. Unfortunately, all that happens to this methane is that it drifts up uselessly to add to the greenhouse effect.

The next most important components of these atmospheric gases are the CFCs, which add to their destruction of stratospheric ozone an effectiveness as greenhouse gases that is about ten thousand times that of carbon dioxide. They contribute about 14 per cent to global warming. A further 6 per cent comes from nitrous oxide (N_2O) produced from fossil fuel burning and by agricultural practices. The remaining 12 per cent is the result of tropospheric (lower atmospheric) ozone, formed largely by the action of sunlight on pollutants from cars and other fossil fuel burning equipment.

The global warming effect was predicted in the nineteenth century, and in 1896 the Swedish scientist Svante Arrhenius stated that use of fossil fuels could double the carbon dioxide in the atmosphere and cause a rise in the average global temperature of about 5 degrees C. He hoped that Sweden might end up with a warmer climate.[13]

In 1957 a carbon dioxide monitoring station was set up on the extinct Mauna Loa volcano in Hawaii as part of International

Human intervention in the carbon cycle, indicated by the annual transfers of carbon (in billion tonnes) between: **a** fossil fuels and atmosphere; **b** biosphere and atmosphere; **c** oceans and atmosphere. The figure at top represents atmospheric carbon, the figures at bottom reservoirs of carbon in recoverable fossil fuels, biosphere, and the surface and deep levels of the oceans (after S. Boyle and J. Ardill)

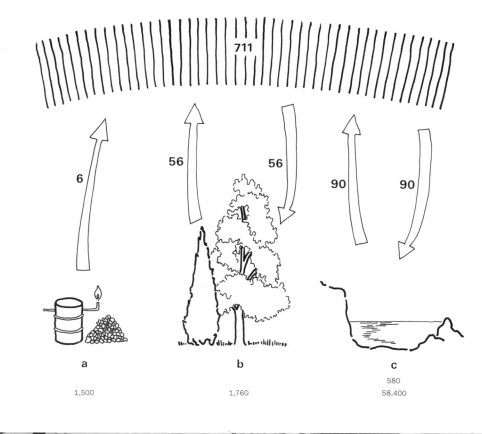

711

6   56   56   90   90

a   b   c

580
1,500   1,760   58,400

The scientist John Dalton collecting marsh gas, otherwise known as the 'greenhouse gas' methane

Geophysical Year. The data from this station over the last thirty years show a steady rise in atmospheric carbon dioxide of 4.5 per cent per decade, increasing in concentration from 315 parts per million to 350 parts per million. The combined effect of all the 'greenhouse gases' by the year 2030 is estimated to be equivalent to a doubling of pre-industrial levels of atmospheric carbon dioxide.

In 1988 climatologists agreed publicly that the greenhouse effect existed, and that it was a real problem. What they do not agree about is the nature of that problem. Differing scenarios predict differing global temperature-rises, from about 4 degrees C to up to 16 degrees C. The effects of such rises, even at low levels, are not easy to predict. Possibilities that have been put forward include a six-metre rise in sea levels due to the melting of the polar ice; the loss of all the world's present grain-growing areas due to shifts and changes in climate; a spreading of the Northern forests – or a destruction of those same forests.

All are agreed, however, that there will be serious effects on land and climate throughout the world. Even a small rise in average sea levels could have a disastrous effect on low-lying countries such as Bangladesh and coastal areas like the Nile Delta. The increasing numbers of natural disasters in the 1980s compared with previous decades are also thought to be due to global warming.

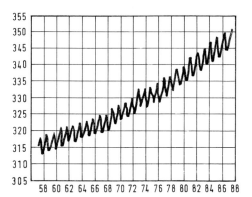

Levels of carbon dioxide in the atmosphere measured at Mauna Loa, Hawaii, 1957–88. Seasonal variations reflect the growth of trees in spring and summer, when they take up more carbon dioxide

The greenhouse effect and the ozone hole are two of the most threatening effects of pollution, but what is their relevance to architects, and those who commission and use buildings? The relevance arises from the fact that roughly 50 per cent of the CFCs produced throughout the world are used in buildings, as part of the air conditioning or refrigeration systems, in fire extinguisher systems, and in certain insulation materials. By careful specifying, architects and others can reduce global CFC use. Similarly, 50 per cent of world fossil fuel consumption is related to the servicing of buildings, therefore 50 per cent of the carbon dioxide output, or a quarter of the total of greenhouse gases, is under the control of the designers or inhabitants of buildings. Provided they demand, or make, environments that use less energy, the greenhouse effect can be slowed down.

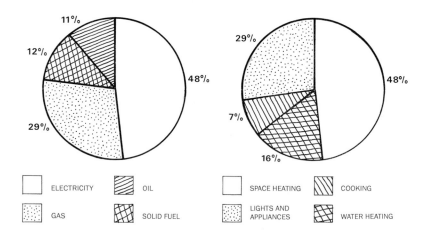

The responsibility of those who design and inhabit buildings for global warming, indicated by carbon dioxide emissions from UK buildings: left, by type of fuel; right, by end use

Water

An undervalued resource

They dumped a can full of trout in the creek and no sooner had the trout touched the water, than they turned their white bellies up and floated dead down the creek.[14]

When fish are found floating dead in rivers and lakes they are visual evidence of the poor quality of the water that surrounds the population. At other times, contamination is not so immediately visible but its effects are no less pervasive.

There is seldom any distinction made between water that is intended to be drunk and water that is used for many other purposes connected with buildings. Buildings use a prodigious quantity of water, both during their construction and during their occupation. The average domestic consumption is 160 litres per head of population per day in the UK and 220 litres per head per day in the USA. The higher figure is accounted for by the larger flushing cisterns used on US wcs. In order to survive, the human body needs only about 1 litre per day, and the average consumption of water in food and drink is about 2 litres per head per day.[15] Domestic consumption in the UK is only one-third of total water consumption, which comes to about 570 litres per head per day.[16] The high total figure is a result of the great quantities of water used by industry and agriculture. For example, a tonne of cement requires for its manufacture 3,600 litres (3.6 tonnes) of water; a tonne of coke for steel-making needs 18,000 litres of water; a tonne of paper uses 270,000 litres, and even a litre of beer needs 9 litres of water for its manufacture.[17] To manufacture a car needs 75 tonnes of water, which would occupy a tank 5 metres by 5 metres by 3 metres, the volume of a small single-storey house. Even the grain for a loaf of bread needs 2.5 tonnes of water for its growth.[18]

Building materials need similarly large amounts of water for their manufacture. Cement uses 3.6 tonnes of water per tonne of dry cement powder, but to make cement into concrete requires additional water, not only for the mixing but for the washing of the aggregates prior to delivery to the site. The manufacture of a tonne of steel uses 300 tonnes of water.[19] Bricklaying and plastering are also large consumers of water on a building site.

Once a building is complete, its water consumption will depend on its function; for example, a steelworks will use more than a crematorium. In domestic and office accommodation the largest single consumer of water is the wc, which uses in its flushing about one third of the total water used by the domestic sector. This is fresh water, purified and safe to drink, which is flushed straight back to the sewers. The uses of water in UK houses are as follows:[20]

	%
flushing wc	32
personal hygiene	28
laundry	9
washing up	9
drinking and cooking	3
watering garden and washing car	6
losses	13

Less than half of these uses need water of drinking quality, yet drinking water is supplied, at increasing cost in resources and land, in order to satisfy them all.

The water to supply these demands comes almost entirely from rivers. Only 3 per cent of the Earth's water is fresh water that could be used for drinking, and two-thirds of this is locked up in the polar ice caps and the glaciers. Only 0.0001 per cent of the Earth's water is in rivers, and this is the part on which people depend for their water supply. The total volume of water in the world's rivers at any time is about 130 cubic kilometres, enough to supply a world population of 5 billion people with 26,000 litres of water each.[21]

Despite this apparent abundance of water, many people in the world do not have a source of pure drinking water. The reason for this is that human activities pollute the very water that is required. The rivers that serve to supply drinking water also receive effluents

Many rivers show obvious signs of pollution; others are polluted but the evidence is invisible. Rivers are the main source of all the world's drinking water

from sewage works, toxic wastes from industry and run-offs of pesticides and fertilizers from farmland. This problem was recognized thirty years ago with the formation of the International Commission for the Protection of the Rhine against Pollution[22] – an *International* Commission because pollution is no respecter of national boundaries.

The oceans have long been regarded as too large to be damaged by human activities, and so are used as a dumping ground for things that are no longer wanted. The sewage from 12 per cent of Britain's population is discharged untreated into the sea[23] and 30 per cent of UK sewage sludge (the remaining solids after sewage treatment) is also dumped at sea. At the same time as the potential fertility represented by this sludge is thrown away, enormous sums are spent on artificial fertilizers to increase crop yields. Much of this fertilizer is wasted because it is not taken up by crops, and it leaches into groundwater supplies and may render drinking water unsafe for bottle-fed babies in certain areas.[24] The fertilizers are made from scarce fossil fuels which could be used for other purposes. The current attitude is one of separating areas of life into precise packages, each with its own internally consistent rules, but with no interaction between the various areas. In a sane world, sewage sludge would be a resource to be used beneficially rather than a waste to be dumped in the sea[25] where it creates further problems.

Most people know of the hydrological cycle in which water is evaporated from the sea by the action of the sunlight, condenses and falls as rain to the ground, where it fills the rivers and flows back to the sea. This solar-powered cycle is the source of all fresh water supplies; but here again human activities are interfering with a natural system. Rain is no longer the pure water source that it once was (although shampoo manufacturers still advertise their products using the image of pure rainwater). The water vapour that evaporates from the sea leaves behind the minerals that have been carried down the rivers, this is why the seas are salt. However, in its passage through the atmosphere the water picks up the pollutants that human activities have pumped into the air. Like the oceans, the

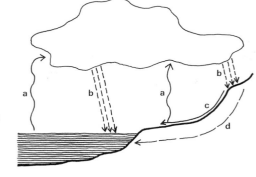

The hydrological cycle:
a Pure water is drawn up into the air as it evaporates from land and sea. **b** It is precipitated as rainfall, becoming acidified as it meets pollutants humans have pumped into the atmosphere. **c**, **d** Water runs off the ground or percolates through the soil, gathering further pollutants as it drains into rivers and thence to the sea

air has for too long been regarded as a sink for wastes. In Britain the infamous London smogs, and in particular the Great Smog of 1952 in which 4,000 people died in five days,[26] led to the passing of the Clean Air Act to control pollution from smoke. However, the combustion of fossil fuels, in particular coal and oil, produces sulphur dioxide, nitrogen oxides and hydrocarbons. These are put into the atmosphere in increasing quantities as global energy consumption rises. In the atmosphere they combine with water to form sulphuric and nitric acids, while hydrocarbons and nitrogen oxides also interact with sunlight to form the tropospheric ozone already mentioned as an atmospheric pollutant. The phenomenon that these substances cause was first referred to as 'acid rain' in 1872 by Dr Robert Smith.[27] Like so many of the current environmental problems, acid rain is not new.

The effects of acid rain are numerous. Architects may perhaps be most concerned by the fact that it dissolves certain building materials. The ancient monuments of Athens have received more damage from pollution in the last twenty-five years than in the last twenty-four centuries.[28] Similar damage is taking place in Krakow, London, Rome, Venice, Cologne, Washington, DC, and other historic cities. Even the Taj Mahal is affected. In countless cathedrals the stained glass is likely to fade within decades. Other constructed systems are not immune: in Katowice, Poland, the railway tracks are so corroded that trains must slow to 40 kph.[29] The US Environmental Protection Agency estimated in 1974 that sulphur dioxide emissions caused 2 billion dollars' worth of damage annually to buildings in the United States.

Serious as these effects undoubtedly are,

they fade into insignificance beside the damage that acid rain is causing to the natural world. The coniferous forests of Europe and North America are suffering increasingly from a phenomenon known as *Waldsterben* (forest death), first noticed as a problem in West Germany in the 1970s following the drought-year of 1976. The problem was at first attributed to the drought, but it worsened, and in 1982 the German government introduced sulphur dioxide emission controls to try to halt the death of the trees. By 1986 87 per cent of the fir trees in West Germany showed signs of damage.[30]

The link between acid rain and *Waldsterben* is still not totally proven, but it is agreed that air pollution is the primary cause of the problem.[31] Acid rain is thought to be the second most important cause in Western Europe.[32] In Britain the Central Electricity Generating Board, the cause of 60 per cent of the country's sulphur dioxide emissions

LEFT AND RIGHT Damaged forests and acid-eroded stone call into question the fashion for out-of-town shopping centres that can be reached only by car

from its coal fired power stations, argued strongly that the link between emissions and *Waldsterben* was not proven. A United Nations report in 1987[33] demonstrated that two thirds of UK conifers showed damage. In June 1988 the UK government committed the country to reducing sulphur dioxide emissions by 60 per cent by the year 2003, and reducing nitrogen oxide emissions by 30 per cent by the year 1998, in line with the European Community directive. It is not known if the forests will recover, or how long recovery might take.

Forests are not the only part of the natural environment to suffer from acid rain. Throughout Europe, Scandinavia and North America the fish stocks in freshwater lakes are being killed by the increasing acidity of

the water. Sweden has 85,000 lakes classified as medium to large, of these 20 per cent are acidified, and 4,000 have suffered serious biological damage.[34] At the end of the last Ice Age, the acidity of Sweden's lakes was pH 7; in many it is now pH 5, which is lethal to the eggs of salmon. Lake Donald in Ontario, once one of Canada's finest places for catching trout and bass, was found in 1973 to have a pH of 3.8.[35]

This appalling type of international pollution may not seem to have much to do with the designers of buildings. However, every tonne of fossil fuel burned, whether burned to heat a building directly or burned in a power station to provide electricity for use within a building, adds further polluting products of combustion to the atmosphere, to be returned to earth in rain. Moreover, the proliferation of building types such as out-of-town shopping centres which depend upon car travel increases the quantity of pollutants to the air from exhaust systems. Architects who condone such building types through designing them must bear some responsibility for the pollutants produced, just as architects who neglect to build energy-conserving buildings bear a responsibility for pollutants from the unnecessary burning of fossil fuels.

Fire

The problem of fuels

And the night-fires going out, and the lack of shelters . . .[36]

Most of the world's activities, from manufacturing cars to preparing a meal in a remote African village, depend on the consumption of fuels, but the kinds and amounts of fuel used in these two activities are vastly different.

The fuels used can be divided into two categories: finite and renewable. The finite fuels are those that are no longer being made – coal, oil, natural gas and uranium. The renewable fuels are those that are derived from natural resources such as solar energy,

wind power, water power and timber for firewood. In the world as a whole, renewable fuels in the form of firewood and hydro-electricity presently provide 21 per cent of total energy consumed.[37] The problem of finite fuel is, as their name suggests, that they come to an end. To use Buckminster Fuller's analogy of 'Spaceship Earth', the finite fuels were put in the Earth's fuel tanks when it was built; when they run out there is nowhere to pull in and say 'fill 'er up'.

There is a great deal of uncertainty concerning the future availability of these fuels, because no one knows the size of reserves awaiting discovery. What is certain is that the easy finds of fuels have been made. The costs of extracting fuels from any newly discovered areas are likely to be high, as can be seen in the history of oil. The oil fields of the Middle East are on land; it is a relatively simple matter to drill down and extract the oil. The newer oil fields of the North Sea required an enormous investment in technology and human life to extract the oil from a hostile environment. The Alaskan oil fields, although on land, are in a similarly difficult environment. The oil from these newer fields is more expensive than that from the older fields because it is more expensive to extract. The same holds true for other fuels, which are either found in increasingly difficult areas, or are in ever lower concentrations, so that greater quantities of material must be processed to produce the same quanitity of fuel.

Arguments over the life of fuel resources can continue indefinitely. In fact, it may be that a particular fuel will never be used up completely, for its use will be more or less abandoned because of price rises. However, if the passengers in a car spend the journey arguing about how much petrol is left in the tank, nothing that they say will alter the point at which they run out of fuel. Estimates of the amounts of fossil fuels remaining vary; the following are based on studies by the Watt Committee on Energy in London:[38]

million tonnes of coal equivalent (mtce)	
coal	11,000,000
oil	510,000
natural gas	320,000

World energy consumption is approximately 10,000 mtce per year, so there is, on a simplistic estimate, fuel to last for 1,200 years at present rates of consumption.

The immediate problem with the fuels at present in use is that they release carbon dioxide into the atmosphere as they burn. As mentioned when considering air pollutants, the atmosphere at present contains more than 700 billion tonnes of carbon, and the world's known fossil fuel reserves contain 7,500 billion tonnes. The carbon input into the atmosphere, which is giving rise to so much concern about global warming, is currently of the order of 6 billion tonnes per year.[39] Clearly if all the fossil fuel reserves were to be burned, almost all the additional carbon would enter the atmosphere, and precipitate disaster. There is no way in which the peoples of the world can use up the fossil fuel reserves without destroying the planet.

Energy is the key problem to be tackled if humanity is to continue living on the Earth. The figures above show that it is no longer possible to follow a policy of 'business as usual', and base continued development on increased fossil fuel use.

The population of the world stood at around 5 billion in 1990. United Nations figures show that even with the most optimistic assumptions about the spread of birth control, the population by 2060 would stabilize at 7.7 billion, an increase of over 50 per cent. Less optimistic assumptions, assuming that people cannot be persuaded quickly to limit family size, show a population of 14.2 billion by the end of the twenty-first century.[40]

Economic development, allowing greater access to health and education services, is seen as the key factor in reducing population growth.[41] However, energy growth is an inescapable part of such development. Current world energy consumption stands at 10 terawatt (TW) years per year (a terawatt year is 1 TW of energy, or 1,000 million kilowatts, operating continuously for a year. It is the equivalent of burning 1,000 million tonnes of coal, so current world energy consumption is 10,000 mtce). If per capita energy use remained at the same levels as today, a world population of 8.2 billion (a mid-range estimate of the possible increase) would need about 14 TW years per year. If the per capita consumption generally rose to the levels currently found in industrialized countries, the global consumption would be 55 TW years per year[42] – and, incidentally, the fossil fuels would all be gone in about two hundred years.

The key problem is to permit 'sustainable development', so that all the peoples of the world can enjoy a reasonable standard of living. The developed world might reduce its energy consumption by 50 per cent through the use of the most efficient processes and technologies, but the developing world would still need to increase its consumption by 30 per cent to sustain the 3 per cent annual per capita growth rates needed. The result would be a world energy consumption of 11.2 TW years per year as compared to the present level of 10 TW years per year, and a corresponding increase in pollution and emission of greenhouse gases.

The onus must therefore be on the developed world to reduce energy consumption. With a mere 24 per cent of the world's population, the developed countries consume 77 per cent of the world's energy, and thereby cause at least 77 per cent of the world's pollution. It is important, also, for the developed world to use its wealth to produce the non-polluting technologies that are needed to permit sustainable development, and then to provide the investment required to establish such systems in the developing world. This is the pollution debt that needs to be paid.

In the United Kingdom, studies have been made to show how energy consumption could be reduced. The first was produced in 1979 by the International Institute for Environment and Development. By detailed examination of the various sectors of the UK economy it showed how total energy demand could be reduced by 22 per cent while the standard of living measured by per capita income doubled.[43] A later report by Earth Resources Research Limited (1983) showed that energy consumption could fall by 50 per cent alongside a threefold rise in material standard of living.[44] Both these reports were based on the assumption that

A small electricity generator on a rocky shore. Wave power is capable in theory of supplying the entire electricity demand of an industrial country surrounded by sea

energy efficiency would be the main driving force. In the ERR scenario, 60 per cent of energy could be provided by renewable sources by the year 2025.

A 1988 report by the UK Department of Energy on renewable energy[45] suggested that 50 per cent of UK energy demand could be met from renewable energy supplies based on wind, wave, solar, biomass and water power. Thus only a 50 per cent reduction in energy demand is necessary to meet all UK requirements from renewable energy. At the same time, about 50 per cent of current energy use is for servicing buildings,[46] an energy use which is under the control of those who design, commission and use buildings. A massive reduction in the energy used in buildings, achieved through a green approach to architecture, could move the UK to a position where energy was no longer generated through burning fossil fuels; and what applies in the UK with its high population density and damp climate applies similarly to the other industrialized nations. All could abandon the need for fossil fuels through a reassessment of current attitudes to buildings.

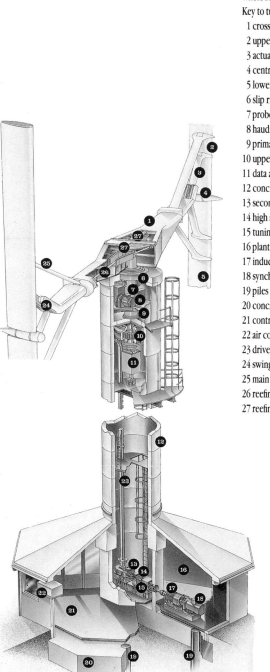

A modern wind-turbine. Wind power is capable of supplying electricity on the scale of a single building or a whole region

Key to turbine:
 1 cross-arm
 2 upper half-blade
 3 actuation strut
 4 centre hinge
 5 lower half-blade
 6 slip rings
 7 probe shaft
 8 haudraulic power
 9 primary brake
10 upper gearbox
11 data acquisition unit
12 concrete tower
13 secondary gear box
14 high speed brake
15 tuning gearbox
16 plant room
17 induction generator
18 synchronous gearbox
19 piles
20 concrete foundations
21 control room
22 air conditioning unit
23 drive shaft
24 swinging link
25 main strut
26 reefing mechanisms
27 reefing actuator

No material is used in building but has its source in the earth. Every use of material involves a transfer of energy, whether more or less expensive. Bauxite ore strip mining (left) is the source of the aluminium used for building components, roofing and cladding

Earth

Resources and materials

Kublai Khan remains silent, reflecting
Then he adds: 'Why do you speak of the
stones? It is only the arch that
matters to me.'
Polo answers: 'Without stones
there is no arch.'[47]

Buildings exist through taking the materials for their construction from the earth, be it stone quarried direct from a stratum of rock or bricks made from baked clay. Smaller structures have often been made from surface soil, whether the adobe of the American southwest or the cob of Devon. Building with earth continued well into the twentieth century even in Britain, home of the Industrial Revolution. A settlement of houses was built at Amesbury in Wiltshire shortly after the First World War by the Ministry of Agriculture to investigate methods of construction that would save scarce and expensive materials. Several different techniques were tried, and the houses are still standing at the time of writing, and are regarded as of high quality.

The Amesbury experiment is a very direct example of building with earth, and for the poorest people this method has the major advantage that the material is free, and only labour is needed to make use of it. However, all the building materials in common use come from the earth in one way or another. Bricks are an obvious example; they are made of burned clay and are really only a slightly more durable version of mud. The same applies to clay roofing tiles. The built environment is no more than a remodelling of the immediate surface of the planet. Timber for building is rooted in the earth, which is needed to grow the trees, although here there is more interaction with air and water as well, and with the pollution-products of fire. The elements in nature are always interconnected.

The Modern Movement in architecture made much play of the use of 'new materials'. Sant' Elia, for example, wrote in 1913:

The house of cement, iron and glass, without carved or painted ornament, rich only in the inherent beauty of its lines and modelling, extraordinarily brutish in its mechanical simplicity, as big as need dictates, and not merely as zoning rules permit, must rise from the brink of the tumultuous abyss . . . [48]

However, whether iron and glass, or the more modern aluminium and plastic, all materials are still won, or more precisely, wrenched, from the earth. The iron ore for steel-making, the bauxite ore for aluminium, the sand from which glass is made, are all extracted from the ground. Additionally, most economically important mineral ores exist in low concentrations, and the process of refining involves concentrating a small component of the excavated material. The spoil is usually left in piles round the mine to form a physical or chemical hazard:

> . . . almost every phase of the process can produce land use changes and environmental contamination: in open-pit mines, to give a single example, the overburden and spoil banks generally exceed the area of the mine by a factor of 3–5 times, and while they provide the raw materials for restoration, they may act as a source of contaminants (dust, silt, nutrients) during their lifetime.[49]

Land is frequently not reclaimed after mineral extraction. Even in supposedly advanced countries it may be allowed to become derelict following mining and other operations:

> The area of land lying officially derelict in England and Wales increased at an average of 2,550 acres (1,032 Ha) annually during the period 1964–71.[50]

Nor is making building materials out of earth a simple matter of digging them up and using them. The processes of extraction, refining, fabrication and delivery are all energy-consuming. The energy used adds its share of pollution in the form of acid deposition and carbon dioxide.

The problem of deciding which building material causes the least global damage is complex. First is the need to consider the direct impact on the environment – is it preferable, for example, to grow coniferous forests for timber or to quarry the landscape for stone for building? In addition, the energy content of any material needs to be considered, for it offers a crude guide to the amount of pollution involved in its manufacture. In general, the low energy materials will be the least polluting (see p.41). However, the choice of a material becomes more complex when the manner in which it is used within the building is considered. Thus, although plastics are high energy materials, as 'plastic' insulation in the form of expanded polystyrene they are light. This lowers their energy density, and when incorporated within the building fabric they will reduce energy demand. Within a year, expanded polystyrene can save five times the quantity of energy that went into its manufacture. Mineral fibre, with a lower manufacturing energy density, can save even more. In addition, the position of the insulating material within the building can affect the choice of type. Although mineral fibre insulation has a lower energy density than expanded polystyrene, it cannot be used to insulate under a concrete slab, where the more energy 'expensive' foamed plastic insulation is required.

Moreover, the choice of a material can be further complicated by other elements used in its manufacture. Extruded polystyrene, a slightly denser and more waterproof foamed insulation, has traditionally been foamed with CFCs, so CFC gas is trapped in each separate bubble within the material. Some manufacturers are searching for less polluting agents for foaming plastics. Chipboard, which is seemingly an excellent material as it uses pieces of waste wood, incorporates a glue in its manufacture which can produce formaldehyde gas inside the building. Although small amounts of such material within a building are unlikely to cause problems, in a building which is reasonably airtight to prevent energy loss through draughts, the gases could build up to an uncomfortable level.

EARTH

1 Dome of the Merdler house, Santa Fe, New Mexico, a solar heated conservatory. The main part of the house is built of the earth on which it stands

BUILDING WITH EARTH

RIGHT, ABOVE
2 An adobe house, King house, Santa Fe, New Mexico, uses the age-old technology of building with sun-dried mud-brick, and the equally ancient technique of collecting solar warmth through south-facing openings

RIGHT, BELOW
3 Rocky Mountain Institute, Colorado, one of the most energy efficient buildings in the world, a home and office with virtually no conventional heating in a climate where winter temperatures can fall as low as minus 40 degrees C. The heavy timber and masonry structure is partly buried in the site and partly earth-covered

OPPOSITE
4 The interior of an underground house by Donald Metz in New Hampshire stores solar warmth in massive inner walls and dense concrete-and-tile flooring. The ornate wood-burning stove is rarely needed

RENEWABLE ENERGY RESOURCES OF WIND AND WATER

LEFT, ABOVE
5 An Australian wind-powered water pump, supplying drinking water without the use of fossil fuels

LEFT, BELOW
6 Glenn Murcutt re-interprets the Australian vernacular of water pump and corrugated steel for the Kempsey Museum, New South Wales. In the heat of the Australian summer the interior spaces of the museum are kept pleasantly cool by currents of air drawn up into the spaces of the double roof and exhausted through large roof ventilators. There is no need for fossil fuels to run the air conditioning

RIGHT
7 The wind array, capable of generating electricity on the same scale as a conventional power station, but with a mere quarter of the carbon dioxide pollution of the 'nuclear option', and safely, without risk of nuclear accident

'FIRE' WITHOUT POLLUTION

INSET, FAR LEFT
8 The technology of direct conversion of sunlight into energy, developed for space exploration, can now provide domestic electricity at point of use. A system of photovoltaic panels is mounted on the roof of a solar house at Carlisle, Massachusetts, to supplement power from the public utility company. Any surplus electricity generated can be fed into the grid

LEFT AND INSET
9,10 Apartments in a solar village near Athens are designed to collect and store the sun's heat with passive and active solar technologies. South-facing glazing, high mass walls and active solar collecting panels reduce energy demand by 80 per cent, compared to conventional apartments. Summer cooling is by north-south cross-ventilation and moveable awnings. The same simple technologies of layout and glazing to maximize solar gains are applied to sheltered housing for elderly people at Bournville, England (inset). Architects: Athens, Alexandros N. Tombazis. Bournville, David Clarke Associates

Cooling and
Warming

11 For a house in Athens, the
concrete components of the
balcony and even the
handrails are carefully angled
to shade the rooms in
summer, but allow the winter
sun to enter when its heat is
needed. Mass materials inside
the building store the
warmth.
Architect: M. G. Souvatzides

Using a heat recovery ventilation system can allow the pollutants produced by chipboard glues to be removed without incurring major energy losses.

The choice of any building timber is also complex. There has been a call for the use of softwoods in preference to hardwoods because of the damage caused to the rainforests. However, the majority of rainforest damage is through clearance to give land for cattle ranching. The need is to encourage the use of hardwoods from managed forests, as this will, in turn, encourage the retention of forests as they become a sustainable source for timber and thereby generate income for the countries of location.

As a rough guide, however, the energy intensiveness of a building material will act as a guide to its 'greenness'.

The energy content of a material is clearly connected to its closeness to the earth; the more it is refined, the more energy it contains. However, it has to be remembered that the figures are in energy content *per kilogram*, and the 'low energy' materials are largely those that are used in bulk. Steel, while high energy, is not a mass material, but one used in carefully sized sections to provide structural efficiency. To judge the energy content of any particular building would require a detailed calculation of the weights of materials used in conjunction with their energy contents. Szokolay offers figures for the energy intensity (again in terms of energy content of materials) of different building types:[51]

	kWh/m²
domestic buildings	1,000
office buildings	5,000
industrial buildings	10,000

These figures can be compared with the annual energy consumption of different building types in use:[52]

	kWh/m² less than
office	195
factory	222
warehouse	195
school	195
shop	195
hotel	361

Attempts have been made to put numerical values to energy intensiveness, so that materials can be ranked.[53]

material	energy content: kWh/kg
Low energy materials	
sand, gravel	0.01
wood	0.1
concrete	0.2
sand-lime brickwork	0.4
lightweight concrete	0.5
Medium energy materials	
plasterboard	1.0
brickwork	1.2
lime	1.5
cement	2.2
mineral fibre insulation	3.9
glass	6.0
porcelain (sanitary ware)	6.1
High energy materials	
plastics	10
steel	10
lead	14
zinc	15
copper	16
aluminium	56

House at Trees Ranch, Utah, built of local stone and timber: fir and cedarwood. A shady porch, mass walls, solar panels and evaporative cooling continue energy savings in operation. Architect: William McDonough

A kilogram of mineral fibre insulation is large in volume compared, for instance, with a kilogram of concrete, and at 3.9 kWh per kg, has a relatively low energy-intensiveness. Since, as the table has shown, the energy content of insulating materials is moderate, their use in quantity will not add appreciably to the total energy consumed in making a building, while their incorporation can bring about a 50 per cent or greater decrease in energy use during the building's lifetime.

It is also evident that energy used to make a building may be as much as that required for ten or twenty years of operation. This points to the need to consider very carefully the life of the building (planning and durability of materials) and the possibility of recycling the materials, were the building to reach the end of its usefulness.

Some architects are making attempts to consider the impact of their choice of materials as widely as possible. At the Findhorn Community in Scotland a group of self-build houses has been designed for minimum ecological impact.[54] All the materials chosen are low energy and non-toxic. The houses are largely constructed of timber from sustainable sources, used untreated or finished with organic paints or wax. The roofs are clay pantiles. The insulation material is cellulose manufactured from recycled newspapers, impregnated with non-toxic boron (boracic acid) to render it fire resistant. It is intended that the hydroscopic properties of the cellulose will draw moisture out of the timber structure and help to preserve the untreated wood. The walls and roofs 'breathe': careful selection of the properties of internal and external cladding allows unwanted water vapour to diffuse through the structure without condensation (usually prevented by a vapour barrier). Everything used in the construction of the houses is biodegradable. Should a house reach the end of its useful life, all its materials can be re-used, or be allowed to rot naturally, without environmental harm.

The techniques of materials-use may help or hinder their long term life through recycling; for instance modern cement mortars adhere so firmly to bricks that the latter will crack rather than separate from them, whereas soft lime mortar as used in the nineteenth century can be easily cleaned from bricks. There is a small industry involved in the cleaning and resale of Victorian bricks in England, but modern brickwork is only useful for hardcore. In the case of larger buildings, a reinforced concrete frame will only be rubble when demolished, whereas a steel frame can be unbolted, re-used, re-welded or melted down and re-formed.

It is no longer sufficient, therefore, to consider the immediate performance of the building fabric, for the eventual re-use of the building's elements once its first purpose has been fulfilled must form part of any green approach towards design. The durability and re-use of buildings (rather than their materials) is considered in more detail in a later chapter.

The built environment, then, relates to earth and water, fire and air, and its interaction with each of these elements is such as to involve the transfer of energy. In a world under threat, each transfer of energy needs to be carefully considered to determine its implications, and whether it is really necessary.

2 PERFORMANCE

Assessing Western patterns of consumption – and their alternatives

In Western society, such everyday actions as turning on the light or setting out for work are performed without thought for their consequences. If it were possible to understand the consequences of these actions in terms of their impact on the environment, it might also be possible to conceive of less harmful ways to achieve the same ends. Heating and lighting, discarding materials or even buildings, and moving between home and work, all have grave consequences. Yet even quite small changes in the way such actions are performed could be enough to bring a sustainable future.

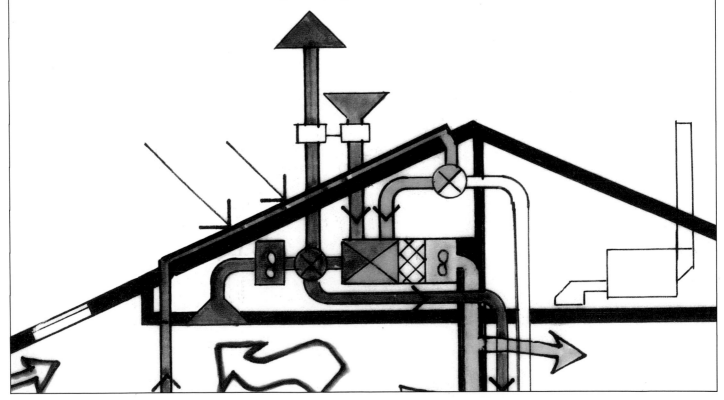

ALTHOUGH the interactions between the built environment and the natural world as represented by the four ancient elements have been shown to be broadly destructive, alternatives do exist. At present these possibilities occur as strands which have not yet been fully linked to form a green web, but at some future time may be so. Nor have matters yet been planned so that connections are formed which might multiply the effect of single efforts. Indeed, the present attitude of many governments in the West is that planning is itself an unnecessary evil, and that problems which are left to the forces of the market will find satisfactory solutions without intervention.

This attitude has been and must again be questioned. As Barbara Ward observed when such issues were considered more than a decade ago:

> For all its immense value as an impersonal indicator of needs and wants in an abundant economy, the market's method of conservation of [scarce resources] is simply to exclude the weak. In a true community, the solution is solidarity and sharing. There is no other choice.[1]

Thus, although the alternatives can be pointed out, it will require more than individual effort if they are to have their full effect. A realization of the problem and the resources in common may form the beginnings of some more fundamental change in attitude which is the necessary precursor to change.

How such change might come about is explored through five ordinary activities that may be performed at the start of any day in the Western world. Alongside the activities, existing alternative strategies are suggested as a basis on which a planned metamorphosis for a sustainable future might be initiated.

Turning on the light

The electric lights in the street cast a
pale sheen here and there on the ceiling
and the upper surfaces of the furniture,
but down below, where he lay,
it was dark.[2]

Franz Kafka: 'Metamorphosis'

Those who have lived, even for a short time, with a Lister 'Start-o-matic' or similar diesel generator will have experienced at first hand the connection between turning on the light and the burning of fossil fuel. Waking in the middle of the night with the desire to go to the bathroom, the unfortunate who turns on the light will hear, somewhere in the distance, the sound of a starter motor and the gradual stirring of the diesel engine into life; then after a suitable interval, the lightbulb begins to glow. After such an experience it may be thought preferable to grope in the

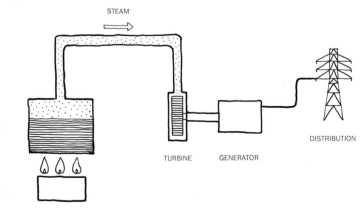

Electricity as an end product. Most conventional power stations use a fuel, usually coal, gas, oil or uranium, to boil water to make steam to drive a turbine connected to the generator that makes electricity for distribution. Each stage of the process involves a loss of efficiency

STEAM

BOILER

TURBINE   GENERATOR

DISTRIBUTION

FUEL

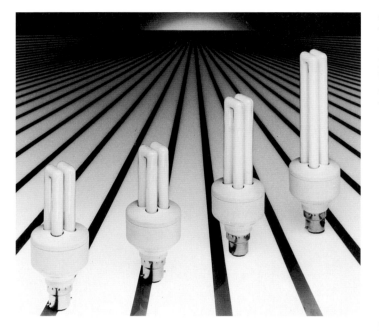

Compact fluorescent lightbulbs, saving four-fifths of the electricity used by tungsten bulbs, and causing one fifth of the pollution

environment. Much has been written about the relationship between the technology of lighting and the development of the deep-plan building and the common assumption is that the technology has produced a welcome development. Reyner Banham, for instance, writes of the deep-plan office building:

> … not only was the clear, well-serviced rectangular floor plan attractive enough for its rents to absorb that extra 8 per cent (the additional cost of the air-conditioning, fluorescent lights and acoustic ceiling, all attributes that were needed by deep plan buildings), but architects had by now more or less unanimously decided that their post-War skyscraper dreams were going to be realized in a starkly rectangular aesthetic.[3]

It matters not whether the image of the prismatic skyscraper provided the impetus for the development of the technology that would make it possible, or whether the technology prompted the development of the

dark, rather than awaken the slumbering monster for such a trivial reason.

The advent of centrally generated electricity has removed the immediacy of this experience from most users of light switches, yet the effect of turning on the light is always and everywhere the same. Somewhere, fuel has to be burned to provide the power to make the lightbulb glow. If it were possible to improve the efficiency of lightbulbs, then it would be possible to reduce the quantities of raw fuel required to light a nation. Such a possibility now exists.

Several manufacturers produce lightbulbs which use fluorescent tubes contained inside a device about the size of a conventional tungsten lightbulb. The new bulbs are a direct replacement for the normal type, but because of the greater efficiency of the fluorescent tube in converting electrical energy to light, the new compact fluorescent lamps use only about one fifth as much electricity as a tungsten bulb for the same light output. In normal domestic use they have a life of at least five years before needing replacement.

The best way to save energy is not to use it at all. Making use of natural daylight in buildings is a first and most obvious step in minimizing the impact of the building upon the

Waste is avoided in an office building with infra-red sensors that turn off the light when no-one is using the space

aesthetic. At no time were the implications of such technology and the buildings it made possible explored in any depth. Only later was it realized that such buildings literally cut off the occupants from the outside world, since no external conditions were registered within the building and few people could have access to a window. Moreover, by the nature of the architecture the human scale that had belonged to the older, notched and stepped-back forms necessary to achieve natural light within the structure was lost. The technology allowed an aesthetic that drew further away from the natural language of shelter that had formed a common basis for so many centuries. In determining the form of the building, the user had become less important to the aesthetic than the technology that runs it.

The first step in any metamorphosis of the use of energy for lighting is to reduce demand through the use of natural light within the structure. If this means that deep-plan buildings are no longer possible, then the aesthetic will change. If, at the same time, the need to bring light into buildings brings the users into contact with the world outside the building, then this would seem a satisfactory solution from the users' point of view.

The natural corollary of more use of daylight within buildings would seem to be for work to begin and end with the day. However, while artificial light is necessary, a green approach to the problem is to consider the ramifications of the use of such lighting.

As mentioned, the technology already exists to provide electric light for a smaller expenditure in electrical energy. The greatest savings of energy are made by replacing tungsten lamps with compact fluorescents, but in commercial and industrial buildings a combination of more careful lighting design and improved lighting technology will show significant savings.

The use of low-energy lightbulbs has ramifications beyond the immediate building user. Every time a tungsten lightbulb is replaced with a low-energy lightbulb, the amount of generating capacity needed by the electricity industry to produce that light is also reduced. An 18 watt low-energy bulb gives the same light as an 80 watt tungsten bulb, making a saving of about 60 watts per bulb. Every bulb replaced therefore reduces the need for power station generating capacity by 60 watts.

To appreciate the economic consequences of saving energy it is necessary to compare the costs of generating a particular amount of energy with the costs of saving a similar amount. The dual aspects of such a comparison are capital and running costs. When capital costs are compared, it is possible to show that a megawatt of power station capacity costs at least twice as much as a 'negawatt of uncapacity', or megawatt saved by the use of

A low-energy office, the Building Research Establishment, Watford, England. Window size is carefully calculated to maximize natural light while avoiding heat loss. Energy use is halved, compared to a conventional office block

low-energy lightbulbs. Moreover, although a megawatt of generating capacity has an additional running cost, through the fuel consumed at a power station to produce it, a similar 'negawatt of uncapacity' has no running costs, since all the costs involved are capital costs. If the capital cost of the power station is added to the running costs, over the life of the station the cost of producing a 'negawatt of uncapacity' is only one-eighth that required to produce a megawatt of capacity. This fact is acknowledged by the electricity generating industry in the USA, where low-energy lightbulbs have been given free to customers by one electricity company as a cheaper alternative to the construction of new power plants.

For the electricity consumer it makes sense to buy low-energy lightbulbs even if they cost fifty times as much as tungsten bulbs. The fact that each lasts over five years, and that during this period each uses only 20 per cent of the electricity used by a tungsten bulb for the same light output, means an overall saving to the consumer of some 50 per cent of the cost of using tungsten bulbs.

If, for example, each of the 20 million housholds in the UK were to use just one low-energy lightbulb in the home, the total saving in generating capacity would be 1,200 megawatts, which is about the capacity of a large power station. As in the USA, it would clearly pay the electricity industry to supply low-energy lightbulbs free to its customers.

When a power station is built, it absorbs all the capital cost during the construction period and then has operating costs for fuel and maintenance. During construction it needs a large workforce who are laid off after eight years when it is finished. No energy is produced by the power station until it is built; all the money is spent before any output is produced. The lightbulb scheme solves all these problems: its administration provides continuous employment because the bulbs will need replacements over the probable forty-year life of the power station; it has no additional running costs, and it does not depend on world availability of uranium or other fuels; savings are made as soon as the first lightbulb is plugged in; and the costs are spread over forty years so there is less need for a large initial investment. People often object to the building of power stations, but it would be hard to object to the receipt of free lightbulbs. Any government that announced the distribution of free lightbulbs rather than the building of more power stations would be certain to improve its chances of re-election.

Because electricity is saved, pollution is reduced, whether by acid rain, carbon dioxide or nuclear waste. At the same time, reserves of finite fuels are saved for other purposes. In a market situation costs are a

The chill Victorian parlour, made habitable by lavish decoration and layers of undergarments. The visual effect of comfort to some degree compensates for its thermal lack

measure of the energy and resources needed for a product, and, as has been shown, this measurement strongly favours the free light-bulb scheme.

The green approach to the action of turning on the light is therefore to question the way in which light is provided. Whether it can be provided from natural sources by the use of windows is a first consideration. At the same time, a window can in some circumstances be a cause of too much heat entering a building, and in others be an agent of accelerating heat loss. A balance needs to be struck by the designer between the economic benefits of natural daylight and the possible economic 'disbenefits' of other energy considerations. Then the existing technologies need to be examined, in a search for more sustainable alternatives.

Turning on the power

He could see through the crack in
the door that the gas was turned on
in the living room ...[4]

For more than a century it has been taken for granted in the West that at least a proportion of the population will have some form of fuel delivered to their homes to enable them to live more conveniently and comfortably. The introduction of piped fuels into houses came towards the end of the Industrial Revolution, at the very point where productive work within the home such as home-based weaving that had led to the development of a particular architecture to provide good daylight

The plain, bare surfaces of the Modern Movement, psychologically suited to warmer climates, or the higher room temperatures brought by central heating

had moved into mills and factories. The newly serviced homes developed a set of domestic technologies based on use of the new power sources and the machinery they made possible. Jobs hitherto done by hand were done by machine and fuel. While machines lightened domestic tasks, the claim that they reduced the overall labour and time spent on work within the home can be seen as a myth:

> In household production too, as else-where, we have shown a tendency to use the time freed by labor-saving machinery not for more leisure, but for more goods or services of the same general character. The invention of the sewing machine meant more garments, for a time gar-ments on which there was an enormous

amount of sewing – tucks, ruffles and so on. The invention of the washing machine has meant more washing, of the vacuum cleaner more cleaning, of new fuels and cooking equipment, more courses, and more elaborately prepared food.[5]

The ready availability of convenient fuels within the home has, in the name of that undefinable concept 'progress', encouraged the increasing use of such fuels without com-mensurate increase in benefit. Physical and even psychological comfort have become equated with the burning of fossil fuels. The Victorian woman relied for comfort chiefly on conservation of bodily heat by the layers of clothing that she wore. Sufficient were her number of undergarments and petticoats for the newly leisured middle-class woman to feel comfortable when seated in an ambient temperature of only 12.5 degrees C, a temperature that could be achieved in a room with one fire burning. Thickly draped windows and generously upholstered seating provided a visual effect of warmth and comfort as well as some insulation. A specific aesthetic developed of patterned surfaces and a preponderance of small objects, as if in answer to the need to feel surrounded with familiar objects to compensate for the cold room. Conversely, it is tempting to speculate that the stripped, bare surfaces of the Modern Movement interior would not have been as widely acceptable as they were without the

ABOVE AND RIGHT
Prefabricated timber-framed Scandinavian house, with a high level of thermal insulation to give comfortable conditions in cold climates. The plan and exterior appearance can be varied as required

RIGHT AND BELOW
A gas-fired condensing boiler,
extracting latent heat from
the water vapour in the waste
flue gas, and the thermostatic
radiator valve, allowing each
room to be set to a different
temperature, and turning off
the radiator when the sun
shines

advent of central heating, giving higher air temperatures within the room and a consequent increase in fuel consumed.

Without suggesting that there should be a return to the age of a multiplicity of petticoats, the simple expedient of conserving body heat rather than burning fuel should be the basis of all domestic architecture in a cold climate. It is a simple approach that countries like Sweden adopted long ago.

If domestic appliances must be accepted as a necessary adjunct to modern living, the very least that can be achieved is an increase in the efficiency of those appliances, so that less fuel is used.

> Detailed engineering studies in Denmark indicate that the energy consumption of typical electric or gas cookers could be reduced by 55 per cent or more at a modest cost, through better insulation of the oven, adjustment to the design of burners or heating elements, superior seals on oven doors and the use of forced convection.[6]

Merely to wash clothes in a machine in cold water rather than hot, a technology that the existing so-called 'low temperature' detergent makes possible, reduces demand on fossil fuels. If every household did one laundry wash in cold water each week, another power station could be closed down. The utility companies exist to sell fuels, and so the onus is on designers and users to seek out from manufacturers the appliances which use fuels most efficiently.

Better technologies already exist to promote the efficient use of energy within the home. For heating, the simple gas condensing boiler can operate at over 90 per cent efficiency; thermostatic radiator valves allow radiators to respond individually to any rise in temperature brought by sunlight or people within the room. Heat recovery systems allow buildings to be ventilated with fresh air, but without a high energy loss. Heat from the exhaust air is transferred to the incoming air at a 60–70 per cent efficiency, although the two streams of air do not mix.

Even something as simple as the choice of

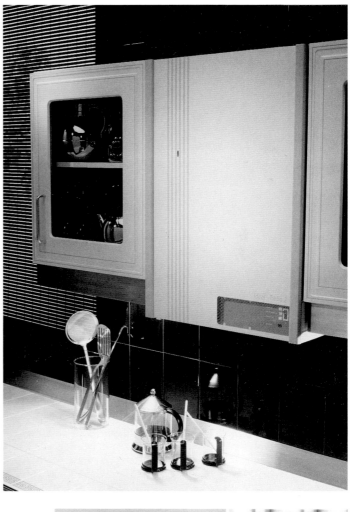

fuel for heating the building has ecological ramifications, both in energy terms and in terms of CO_2 production.

For example, to supply coal with an energy content of 1 kilowatt hour (kWh) needs 0.02 kWh of primary energy. This is the energy needed to work the mine, extract and clean the coal and transport it to the user. Therefore one kWh of coal delivered to the consumer represents 1.02 kWh of primary energy, which is a primary energy efficiency of 98 per cent. The various fuels have different primary energy efficiencies, depending on the complexity of the process used to make them.

	%
electricity from fossil fuels	27
manufactured smokeless fuels	71
synthetic natural gas (estimate)	79
oil	93
natural gas	94
coal	98
wood	99

The amount of energy used will also depend on the efficiency of conversion at point of use. An electric fire is 100 per cent efficient in turning electricity into heat, for example, but the overall efficiency of conversion will still be no greater than 27 per cent.

Fuels also need to be evaluated in terms of the carbon dioxide they produce in combustion:

> Burning coal produces nearly twice as much carbon dioxide per unit of energy obtained as does burning natural gas, while oil lies between the two.[7]

Thus a consumer might select natural gas, where available, as the fuel that produces the least carbon dioxide, and avoid heating a house by electricity where that electricity comes from burning coal, rather than as hydro-electricity.

Nuclear energy is one option that has been proposed.[8] Since nuclear power stations produce electricity without burning fossil fuels, the argument goes, they will not produce any

carbon dioxide, and so will not contribute to the greenhouse effect. The facts of the case are rather different. Uranium, the fuel of nuclear power stations, although not strictly a fossil fuel since it is not derived from the prehistoric remains of living creatures, is nevertheless a finite resource. It is suggested that reserves will become inadequate to meet estimated requirements by 1995.[9]

Moreover, electricity generation accounts for only about 20 per cent of total CO_2 emissions and is, therefore, responsible for only 10 per cent of global warming. To replace all current and planned coal fired power stations up to the year 2020 would require the construction of one 1,000 MW nuclear power station every 1.61 days, a target that is patently beyond the most mechanized building industry. Were this goal achieved, it might reduce global warming by up to 35 per cent, but the cost would be ten times as great as investing in energy-efficient technology to achieve the same result.

Lastly, nuclear power is not a non-CO_2 option. Fossil fuels are used in the whole nuclear cycle, from the mining and enrichment

A nuclear power station – not, as is sometimes suggested, a carbon-dioxide-free option of the uranium fuel to the building of the power station itself. A typical nuclear power station produces on average over its life 230,000 tonnes of CO_2 per year. For all these reasons, it is hard to envisage a future where the energy supply is achieved through nuclear power. Moreover, the disaster at Chernobyl has shown the potential of nuclear power for polluting the natural environment on a global scale.

Possible alternatives to both nuclear and fossil fuels are the use of the natural resources of sun and wind. At the scale of the built environment these are the resources that seem most likely to serve individual buildings. Other sources, such as wave power, hydro power, geothermal power or power from tidal barrages, are more likely to be developed at a scale that would replace conventional power stations. Only in certain geographical circumstances such as occur in Iceland can such power be utilized directly in buildings.

Of the two resources of wind and solar power, wind generators to produce electricity can operate at a variety of scales, from that required to supply a single building to a size or an array that approaches the scale of a conventional power station. Even wind energy, however, is associated with the production of CO_2 during the manufacture of the plant. It has been calculated that wind turbines with an equivalent electricity output to a nuclear power station would produce 54,000 tonnes of CO_2 per year, a quarter of that produced by the nuclear option.[10]

A wind energy array requires considerably more land than a nuclear power station of the same size. This is because the turbines must be a certain distance apart to prevent aerodynamic interference. However, the turbines, access roads, control buildings and other equipment use up very little of the land surface, and the remainder may be used for agriculture with no difficulty. Cows may graze right up to the base of a wind turbine with no worries about radioactive milk. Finally, if a wind turbine in one of these

Wind turbine array. At a capacity equivalent to a nuclear power station it will create only a quarter of the carbon dioxide pollution

arrays suffers an accident, there are two clear advantages. First, the other turbines in the array can continue generating without the need to shut down the whole system, and second, the failure of a wind turbine does not mean the evacuation of a whole region.

Wind power cannot be developed on any large scale as a substitute for conventional power sources without investment. Nonetheless it is used in many different parts of the world and in many different cultures, where it has been proving a reliable source of power for many years. Whereas the nuclear programme in Britain was sold to the population as a technology that would provide electricity so cheaply that it would not be worth metering it, wind power has always been presented as more expensive than the alternatives. That 'free' nuclear electricity has in the end proved so expensive that its continued use has to be subsidized by the State might suggest that the cost of wind energy could be worth examining again.

For the designer of buildings, solar energy is the most suitable renewable source for exploitation. Traditionally solar energy has been used for heating buildings either passively through large glazed areas or actively by heating water or air in solar collectors

LEFT AND BELOW RIGHT Photovoltaic panels used for outdoor lighting, saving on both power and wiring costs. Surplus power can be stored in a battery for use on cloudy days or at night

Photovoltaic cells powering a space station

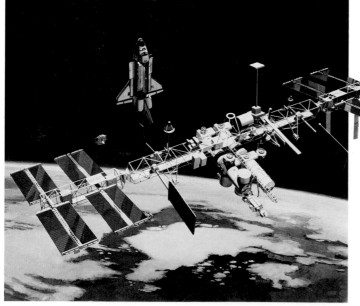

for circulation around the building. The use of solar energy involves storage, either in the building fabric or in separate tanks of water or rock-filled bins. Solar energy can also be used as a power source within buildings through the use of photovoltaic cells. Space stations made use of solar generated power but the costs of the equipment at first prevented the widespread use of the technology for buildings. Japanese researchers have combined electricity generation with roofing by incorporating solar cells in tiles, each tile interlocking with its neighbour to complete a circuit that can be linked back to the grid once the roof is complete. Most examples of the use of photovoltaic cells in buildings are in the USA. Here:

. . . including Alaska and Hawaii, PVs [photovoltaics] now electrify a few thousand

RIGHT
Intercultural Center,
Georgetown University,
Washington, DC, a building at
the leading edge of solar
technology. The vast, 3,250-
square-metre roof is covered
with photvoltaic panels
capable of producing 300 kW
of electricity on a sunny day.
The Center is part of a
strategy to make the whole
University self-sufficient in
electricity by the year 2000

remotely located homes and thousands of remote facilities such as microwave stations, railroad signals, and harbour navigation lights. Five major PV power plants are now operated by US utilities, with two more on the drafting board.[11]

The advantage of a photovoltaic electric generating system is that the electricity can be generated at point of use, without need for transmission lines. Some form of storage is required within the building, usually in the form of batteries; or the building can be connected to the grid in the normal way, and the photovoltaics be used to supplement the normal electricity supply. The photovoltaic cells continue to generate even in overcast skies, although such conditions may reduce their generating capacity by as much as 70 per cent. The technology does exist to provide power within the home and workplace from renewable sources of energy, with a consequent reduction in pollution of the environment.

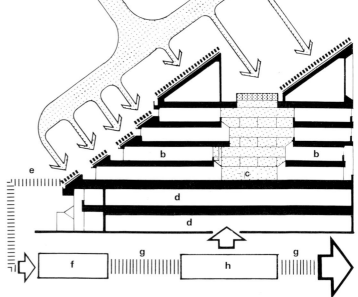

Section of Intercultural
Center:
a solar radiation on to
photovoltaic cells;
b offices; **c** atrium;
d classrooms;
e direct current;
f phase inverter;
g alternating current;
h campus grid, supplying the
Center and other buildings

Waste as a resource

... For this reason many things could
be dispensed with that it was
no use trying to sell but that should
not be thrown away either.[12]

Waste is a concept that passes largely unquestioned in the West except during those periods when the mechanisms for its removal break down. During a strike of refuse-collectors the streets may fill with rubbish, but nature will also move in, through the presence of vermin and the bacteria and microflora and fauna of decomposition, in order to attempt to complete the cycle of disposal. The natural world knows no waste, but only continuous cycles of decay and regeneration, with the same elements passing through these cycles in many different forms.

Just as gardeners who are in sympathy with nature have defined a weed as no more than a plant in the wrong place, so pollution could be redefined as a waste-product in the wrong place. Up to a point this definition holds, but manufacture has been responsible for the production of some synthesized products that cannot be assimilated by the environment so easily. The World Commission on Environment and Development reported in 1987:

> In many cases the practices used at present to dispose of toxic wastes, such as those from the chemical industries, involve unacceptable risks. Radioactive wastes from the nuclear industry remain hazardous for centuries. Many who bear these risks do not benefit in any way from the activities that produce the wastes.[13]

The built environment is associated with waste production in a number of ways. As discussed earlier, the designer or user who fails to implement energy-conserving measures will be placing 'waste' carbon dioxide into the atmosphere without regard to the consequences. Because it is invisible it is easy to ignore it. Similarly, the preferred method of solid waste disposal in the Western world has

Methane gas from decomposing garbage (top) has found an application as fuel to fire kilns at a brickworks (centre). No one has yet found a means of collecting the methane gas emitted by a herd of cows

been burial, another instance of the 'out of sight, out of mind' approach. Unfortunately the nature of the ordinary refuse of the built environment is to decompose when it is buried, with the production of what is known as 'landfill gas'. This gas is mainly methane which is inflammable, and as mentioned previously, is a significant contributor to the greenhouse effect. To protect the public, mains and collecting pipes have to be laid as the tip is filled and the collected gas is burned off. However, accepting that rubbish will continue to be disposed of in this way, it is still possible to make use of the output.

The cycle of waste generation and disposal has been elegantly closed at a brickworks in the north of England. Any brickworks generates large holes within the landscape as the clay is removed for brickmaking. Such holes have often been the site of amenity reclamation schemes once all the clay is extracted. However, in this instance the holes have been rented by the brickworks to the local authority for use as landfill sites. During the process of rubbish disposal by the local authority, collecting mains for landfill gas are laid within the waste. Once decomposition provides sufficient gas, the gas generated supplements the natural gas used to fire the brick kilns, or even replaces it totally in some circumstances. The brickworks, therefore, reduces its dependence on fossil fuels (natural gas), does not duplicate the pollution of combustion (since the landfill gas must be burnt off for safety), and returns the landfill site to a much safer condition at the end of the process.

The wastes that collect at a typical sewage treatment works can also be broken down to produce methane, and in some locations, as at Cambridge in England, this gas is used as the fuel for generators that provide the electricity to run the treatment works. Such systems, however, are not applicable at the scale of individual buildings.

At the domestic scale, the composting of sewage and waste can be carried out successfully. In Sweden and Denmark in particular, several types of composting w c are available commercially, and provide a useful source of garden compost when emptied about once in every two years. The units are quite large, however. Electrically heated models are available which are smaller and can be used in a conventional bathroom, but there is an energy penalty.

Household waste incineration has been used to generate heat for use in a city, a further example of the fuel possibilities created where a centre of population and industrial processes are in proximity. Of the 130,000 tonnes per year of domestic refuse generated in Sheffield, England, approximately 25 per cent go to landfill, but the remainder is incinerated. The following table gives the estimated calorific value of the refuse:[14]

	% by weight	BTU/lb	KJ/kg
Screenings below 2 cm	12.31	307.78	717.13
Vegetable and putrescible	35.46	871.88	2031.48
Paper	31.12	1900.62	4428.44
Metals	5.34	–	–
Textiles	1.70	113.78	265.11
Glass	9.31	–	–
Plastics	2.97	486.49	1133.52
Unclassified	1.79	139.93	326.04
Gross calorific value		3820.48	8901.72
Nett calorific value		3285.20	7655.72

In 1984–5 about 100,000 tonnes of trade and domestic refuse were incinerated, producing sufficient heat for more than 2,500 nearby council-owned properties. The incinerators are linked to conventional steam-raising boilers which are in turn connected to steam-to-high-pressure-hot-water heat exchangers, from where the heat is taken through insulated mains to the neighbouring apartment blocks. The flue emissions are cleaned since the incinerator operates in the centre of a city which is a clean air zone. A central location for the non-polluting incinerator reduces the travel-distance of refuse disposal vehicles, thereby further reducing pollution and costs. The costs involved for this method of waste disposal, when adjusted for the value of the heat generated, are half those for conventional landfill. The environmental impact of this method of waste disposal is much less.

Other types of waste material have been used in the heating of a single building. The Neopit Elementary School, Wisconsin, uses waste wood scraps in place of conventional fossil fuels. The waste wood is delivered into a circular concrete silo buried underground, and an auger feeds it automatically to the burner. Although burning wood will put carbon dioxide into the environment, it is the displacement of a conventional fuel with waste that reduces the overall burden. Even were the waste wood allowed to rot naturally, the quantity of carbon dioxide that passed into the atmosphere would be no less than that produced by combustion for heating. It is also perfectly possible to devise plant for

RIGHT
Straw, generally viewed as an
inconvenient waste-product
of agriculture, can be
converted into useful
building boards for partitions
and interior linings

such operations that does not put further dangerous products of combustion into the atmosphere, either by ensuring complete combustion or through the use of catalytic converters in the exhaust line. It has been estimated[15] that in the UK some 2 million tonnes of waste wood are produced annually and this could be used to heat some 5 per cent of the housing stock, were the houses to be reasonably insulated.

Rather than burning wastes to heat buildings, designers can specify materials made from waste in preference to virgin materials. A whole industry has developed around the use of small wood particles in chipboards, blockboard and fibre boards, and such materials can be used as substitutes for timber in plank or other form. They are also cheaper than the natural alternatives. However, while these products will be preferred by the green designer as being made of otherwise useless materials, some of the particle-boards give off potentially harmful gases from the glues that are used to bond the wood chips together. Although a small amount of chipboard-based furniture is unlikely to cause harm in a normal house, if such materials are used in an airtight environment such as might be associated with energy conservation, high levels of such gases can build up in the indoor atmosphere. Where heat recovery ventilation systems are incorporated into energy conserving buildings, the problems are reduced. It is necessary to consider the particular circumstances before deciding to use such materials.

Other agencies have attempted to make different uses of waste as part of the buildings themselves. In the post-war period when conventional materials were in short supply, it was suggested that straw bales should be used, not only as a fuel, as they are on some farms today, but also as a convenient insulating building-block. Such uses of straw are obviously preferable to burning in the field. In contrast, the ECOL house (ecology + building + common sense) designed and built at McGill University in Montreal in 1972 used waste sulphur as a building block. The sulphur was itself a by-product of the exploitation of fossil fuels:

The last few years have seen a new 'mining' of sulphur as the petroleum industries, being required to de-sulphurize natural gas and petroleum, have become major sulphur producers, to the point where 30 per cent of the world's sulphur is produced this way.[16]

The sulphur was utilized by melting it and mixing it with warmed sand and plasticizers to make a sulphur concrete. The mixture was then poured into moulds to form an interlocking block which could be constructed into a wall without any mortar. Once the first course of blocks at ground level had been laid straight, the remainder of the wall could be stacked with the minimum input of skilled work. Such a system, it was hoped, would be useful for user-built housing in the Third World, since the cost of the walling material, using as it did a waste product, and the skilled labour required were both minimal.

The proposal to make building blocks of waste may be taken seriously in the West, not so much to provide alternative uses for waste

materials as to provide a way of cleaning land which has been poisoned with dumped toxic chemicals. A Texas company has recently developed a technique of uniting contaminated soil and sludge with cement and other chemicals to form a concrete-like substance that prevents the toxic chemicals leaching out into surrounding ground water:

> The additive changes the chemistry of the cement to an almost impermeable matrix that creates its own moisture barrier . . . A mass of toxic dirt from a construction site can be processed and repoured into the ground for a foundation far better than the poured-in-place concrete normally used . . .[17]

Such was the toxicity of the wastes to be re-used that the ground would otherwise have been unacceptable to build upon. The future building block of recycled chemicals may be far removed from the simple sulphur technology demonstrated in the ECOL house.

Rather than merely making use of wastes in building materials as a reaction to waste producing situations, it has sometimes been proposed that products should be specifically designed so that at the end of their first life they can have a further use as building-components.

Many developing peoples have already learned to make use of the waste products of richer societies. In view of the high cost of building materials, a logical step would seem to be the design of short-lived products specifically for re-use as building blocks. The idea of making a bottle that could later be used as a brick occurred to the Dutch brewer Alfred Heineken in 1960:

> During his visit [to Curaçao] Heineken, like every other traveller, saw the *bidon-villes* and deplored the living conditions they revealed. He also saw that empty Heineken bottles littered the island. In Holland . . . the trucks which deliver crates of beer return to the brewery with empties ready for sterilizing and refilling. Every Dutch Heineken bottle makes an average of thirty or more 'trips' before

laid horizontally with the neck of one bottle fitting into the base of the one adjoining. The bottles were bonded like bricks in sand and cement mortar with a silicone additive. A summerhouse of such construction was built by Heineken in 1965. Patents were filed, but the idea proceeded no further than these experiments. It is perhaps one thing to be so poor that waste materials have to be used for building, another to design specifically for those who must build with rubbish or not build at all.

The Western images of spectacular, motorized, automated, suburbanized consumption that pour from magazines, films, television screen and posters bestride the Third World like a colossus. They have established very clear ideas in the minds of poor people of the kind of housing that they want.[19]

If the WOBO had first found a use in the West its future use elsewhere would have been more promising. It needed to be conceived as a building material that might be

Waste sulphur blocks used for a habitable small building, the ECOL house at McGill University, Montreal. The raised device is an eye-level solar cooker. The chair of the visiting designer-engineer Buckminster Fuller rests on the sulphur-block flooring

BELOW
Drop City, Colorado, built of panels cut from the roofs of scrapped cars and vans. The pre-painted panels are folded over at the edges, bolted together and the joints waterproofed with sealant

being lost or destroyed. Almost all bottles exported on the other hand make only one 'trip'; their contents gone, they become valueless in all but the nuisance their disposal problem creates.[18]

Together with John Habraken and the research division of the brewery, Heineken developed the WOBO (WOrld BOttle), a flattened rectangular container which could be

Heineken's specially designed WOBO beer bottles, re-used as a house-wall

delivered to site containing a useful liquid rather than as a waste product that might just be useful for building. It is only those who have chosen to reject the values of the first world, without necessarily abandoning its wealth, who view wastes as potential building materials:

> We learned how to scrounge materials, tear down abandoned buildings, use the unusable. Culled lumber. Railroad ties. Damaged insulation. Factory-reject plywood. Car tops. The garbage of America.[20]

It is in the first world that the concept of 'waste' needs to be redefined until, as in the natural world, there are no wastes, only further stages in the continuous cycle of use, decay and regeneration. This applies equally at the scale of the individual material and the whole building, where planning for re-use could form part of the parameters of design (see pages 107–127).

Food production

The breakfast dishes were set out on
the table lavishly, for breakfast
was the most important meal
of the day . . .[21]

There is a tacit understanding that food is
more important than shelter and is a need
that has to be satisfied first. However, the
production of food has an essential impact on
the environment, and also of necessity im-
pinges upon architecture through the need
to balance town or city with countryside. It
therefore seems relevant to consider the relationship between the food on the plate and
the built environment.

The Brundtland Report (1987) suggests
that by the turn of the century nearly half the
world's population will live in urban developments. The rise in city living has been
dramatic in the developing world:

Over only 65 years, the developing
world's urban population has increased
tenfold, from around 100 million
in 1920 to 1 billion today. In 1940,
one person in 100 lived in a city of
1 million or more inhabitants; by 1980,
one in 10 lived in such a city. Between
1985 and the year 2000, Third World
cities could grow by another three-quarters of a billion people. This would suggest that the developing world must, over
the next few years, increase by 65 per
cent its capacity to produce and manage
its urban infrastructure, services, and
shelter merely to maintain today's often
extremely inadequate conditions.[22]

In the first world urban development has
been sustained by energy from fossil fuels,
for without such energy it would not be possible to transport the food to the population.
Energy is also required to grow the food, for
as decreasing numbers of people work on
the land they are replaced by machinery
which needs external fuelling. Moreover,
manufacturing the machinery requires

energy, as does the processing and packaging
of food to enable it to be transported. As
increasing numbers of people live in cities,
so the demand for fuel must rise, or else the
way in which food is provided for cities must
change. The problems concerned with
increasing use of fossil fuels have already
been outlined. Any increase in agricultural
activity that relies on these existing technologies can only exacerbate pollution.

Obviously a return to the zero energy im-
plication of an agricultural system such as
hunter-gathering is not reconcilable with
increasing numbers of urban dwellers.
However, the replacement of human labour

Urban cultivated land has
been shown to be more
productive, area for area, than
land under conventional
Western agriculture

by machinery in agriculture has already gone beyond the point where it can show an energy benefit:

For example, one man working on the land has been replaced by an annual consumption of about nine tons of oil. In the twenty years or so up to World War II, this led to a simultaneous release of about three acres (1.5 Ha) of land, because with the man went his horse. Therefore, until the end of World War II, we received a return of useable land for the consumption of oil which replaced the man. There was thus an additional

area for trapping the solar radiation which was necessary to provide food.

Now replacement of men provides no such return, has no biological purpose, and is dictated solely by consideration of short term conventional economics.[23]

To create a sustainable balance between city dwellers and the agricultural land that supplies them, in the developing world and the first world, an alternative needs to be realized to an agriculture dependent on fossil fuels.

The search for such an agriculture has a bearing on the built environment at different scales. It has been suggested that the individual dwelling should be provided with sufficient land for each household to grow its own food.[24] Further self-sufficiency could be achieved through the collection of the income energies of sun and wind. The revolutionary cry of 'Three acres and a cow' may bring with it the seeds of a different way of organizing production and consumption.

Such a suggestion, however, negates the idea of built urban environment in favour of decentralized communities that may in turn increase demand for transport. However, systems operating on such principles, like pre-industrial and Chinese farming systems, can be shown to be much more efficient in terms of the energy input for the food energy output.[25]

As limits to the burning of fossil fuels may be set because of increasing concern about global warming, so the measure of agriculture efficiency may be returned to output per minimal fuel input, or output per hectare, rather than the spurious measure of output per agricultural worker.

The effects of such a change would become visible with the redistribution of population, as more people moved to work on non-energy-intensive agricultural systems. Such farming would provide a countryside that looked more varied than that of today, with more areas of land set aside as natural habitat. Increased numbers of people working on the land would also alter the nature of rural settlements, as a larger permanent population would replace the present dormitory population in many rural villages, and such a permanent population would require its own infrastructure of schools, health care and other services, and the people to run them. In addition, organic crops require access to an immediate market (since they are not treated with chemicals to allow them to withstand transportation, handling and storage before sale). Foods would become localized and regionalized: characteristics which people will now travel to find, to replace the cloned food that is offered in many towns and cities. Such decentralization would also have implications for energy supply. At present, central supplies of energy service centralized populations, but renewable energy supplies, such as solar and wind, operate at low energy densities over wide areas, and may be more appropriately used at a decentralized scale. The political implications of such autonomous regionalized communities may have to become part of any serious move to reduce fossil fuel energy consumption in the developed world.

Street market in Grenoble, France, selling fresh, locally produced food

The journey to work

O God, he thought, what an exhausting job I've picked on! Travelling about day in, day out.[26]

Industrialization separated home from the place of work so thoroughly that today in the first world the home is often an empty place during the hours of daylight, a repository for the products of consumerism, and the workplace correspondingly increases in importance in the life of most people. Such centralization of the activities that lead to production brings with it the need to move perpetually from the one place to another.

ABOVE
Modern, efficient, attractive urban public transport, to tempt commuters away from their cars

RIGHT
Energy consumed by various forms of transport, in megajoules per person per 100 km travelled

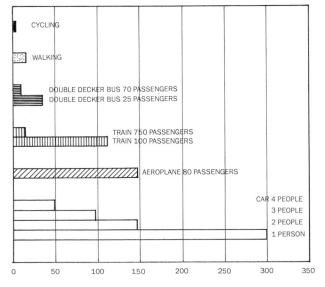

Increasingly, this movement is achieved less by human power and more through the use of fossil fuels consumed in private cars.

In the days before the motor car there was a simple and direct relationship between travel and horsepower: one person, one horse. A modern motorist in even quite a modest vehicle may have the power of fifty or sixty horses under the bonnet in order to make a brief journey. Traffic congestion in major cities is such that the average door-to-door speed of commuting journeys is no greater than that of a person on horseback. Yet a twenty-mile round-trip journey to work may use about 50 kWh of energy per day, or 12,000 kWh per year, as much energy as would heat an average three-bedroom house. As a consequence the private car has become a major source of pollutants in the first world. In Europe, cars and trucks account for two-thirds of carbon monoxide and nearly half of nitrogen oxide emissions. They also produce considerable quantities of carbon dioxide. In consuming 50 litres of petrol a typical European car will produce about 150 kg of carbon dioxide, 9 kg of carbon monoxide and 3 kg of a mixture of oxides of nitrogen and unburnt hydrocarbons. Carbon monoxide prevents the blood from absorbing oxygen, while oxides of nitrogen form nitric acid in the atmosphere, increasing the acidity of rainwater.

Private cars are also an extraordinary convenience, and one which people are anxious to acquire and reluctant to give up. With the use of three-way catalytic convertors attached to exhaust systems combined with improved engine-management techniques, the carbon monoxide, nitrogen oxides and unburnt hydrocarbons can be reduced to negligible levels. These techniques are widely used in many countries, having been pioneered in the USA. In West Germany there were considerable tax concessions to the buyer of a catalytic car, consequently in 1988 only 3 per cent of sales were of non-catalytic cars. Road tests show modern catalytic cars to have fuel economy and performance as good as those of less clean models and, since the catalyst must use unleaded fuels, there is the further benefit of removing lead from the air.[27]

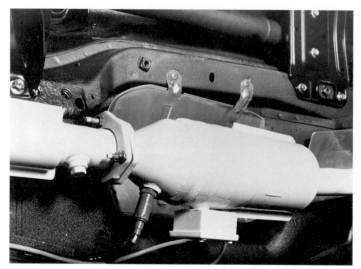

TOP
General Motors Impact electric car, the first electric vehicle to rival the performance of the petrol-driven car

ABOVE LEFT
A catalytic converter fitted to a car's exhaust

However, the catalyst has no effect on the production of carbon dioxide. To avoid CO_2 production, cars could run on batteries charged with a renewable form of electrical energy such as solar, wind or wave power. (The proposed electric-powered conventional cars only shift the production of CO_2 from the street to the power station.) The proposed hydrogen-powered vehicles are only pollution free if the hydrogen is generated by the electrolytic decomposition of water into hydrogen and oxygen using wind, wave or solar electricity. Neither of these alternative means of propulsion will provide cheaper personal transport than exists at present.

The only present answer to the problem of the thermal and chemical pollution produced by cars is to use them less, with an

ABOVE AND LEFT
The hydrogen-powered car, storing the liquid gas in a vaccuum insulated tank inside the baggage compartment. No carbon dioxide is produced in operation, but the hydrogen must be produced by renewable energy if the technology is to have an impact on global warming

DEZE WITTE FIETSEN WORDEN DE BEZOEKERS
GRATIS TER BESCHIKKING GESTELD VOOR HET
MAKEN VAN EEN FIETSTOCHT IN HET PARK.

WIJ VRAGEN U DE FIETSEN NA GEBRUIK
ONBESCHADIGD OP DEZE PLAATS TERUG TE
BRENGEN.

White bicycles in Holland, free for anyone to use as required

inevitable impact on the way the built environment is organized. The journey to work is one of the most wasteful examples of motoring, with a single person in a four- or five-seater car occupying road and parking space.

The first alternative that has been shown to work in some locations is the construction of the built environment around a public transport system sufficiently attractive for people to prefer it to driving. Trams have particular advantages in this respect, as most European cities have long demonstrated. As well as having the potential to use electricity from renewable sources, such transport systems benefit the large number of people who do not have access to a private car.[28]

The other advantage of the construction of the built environment around a system of public transport is a decrease in the energy used, of whatever form, for specific passenger-miles travelled. The table on p. 65 gives values for the transport energy consumed in megajoules per person per 100 km for various methods of travel.[29] Even a car carrying four passengers uses more energy per person carried than a double decker bus travelling less than half full. However the statistics are examined, an environment based on a reduction of energy use must embrace access to public transport as a priority, and do all possible to discourage the use of the private car.

Of all the modes of travel, the least energy intensive is by bicycle or on foot. If home and work or home and school were to be so positioned that the journey could be achieved on foot, then energy use must fall. Yet just at a time when environmental problems are forcing another inspection of accepted patterns of energy use, the built environment is increasingly fragmenting into large functionally determined chunks: the retail park; the industrial park; the leisure complex; the business park. Even within the zones it may no longer be possible to drive to the shopping centres, park, shop on foot and then drive home: the consumer has to drive between a number of scattered specialist locations within the retail park to make his or her purchases.

The present pattern of decentralization combined with agglomeration of like facilities does nothing to further the established traditions of living in cities, the traditions around which the city form developed. Much current development suburbanizes the city

as surely as the inter-war housing estates so reviled by designers.[30] Even information technology systems which should encourage a closer link between home and work without need for travel are all developed in one place: in 'silicon valleys' separate from home and other facilities.

Just as architecture students are occasionally put in wheelchairs to experience the problems of those who are forced to use them every day, so perhaps should designers be forced to live without a car for a month, to allow them to anticipate the frustrations of the inevitable day when an energy tax or traffic congestion brings private transport to a final halt. Without such an insight, the metamorphosis of the journey to work may be a long time coming.

3 PRACTICE

Design in action

Many buildings have some attributes which may be described as 'green'.
Few in the West are entirely benign in their effects on the environment.
In order, therefore, to demonstrate a green architecture, it is necessary
to fragment the holistic green approach, and examine a range of
buildings that each have one or several green features. Six principles are
proposed that together could build into a green architecture.

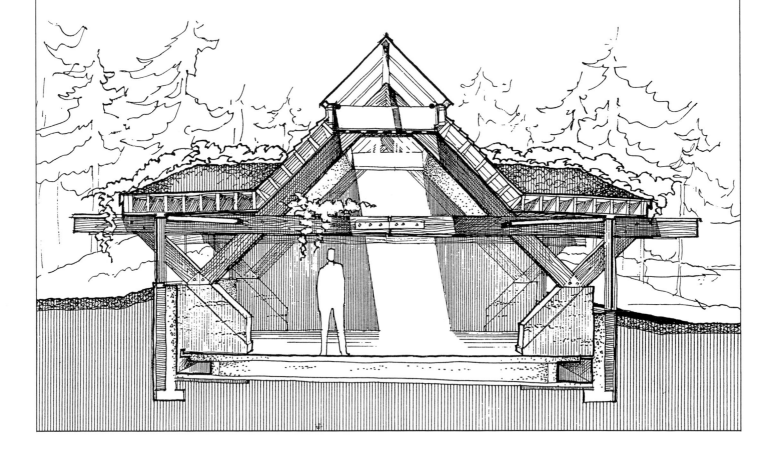

THE 'green' approach to architecture is not a new approach. It has existed since people first selected a south-facing cave rather than one facing north to achieve comfort in a temperate climate. What is new is the realization that a green approach to the built environment involves a holistic approach to the design of buildings; that all the resources that go into a building, be they materials, fuels or the contribution of the users, need to be considered if a sustainable architecture is to be produced. Many buildings embody at least one of the various identifiable green characteristics. Few as yet embrace the holistic approach.

Rather than suggesting ideal or imaginary solutions to the problems of green architecture, a series of buildings will be examined which all embody some green characteristics, considered in relation to a set of green principles. However, the green principles proposed are not intended as a set recipe that must be followed, but are put forward as a reminder of the issues that many designers ignore. The examples chosen may not be the most thorough-built demonstration of each principle, but they have been selected to show the range of solutions that exist, in many different parts of the world. All accord with the underlying green ethic, that to be considered beautiful the object must answer its fundamental purpose well.

Because the 'green' argument is to suggest that issues are interdependent, and that the ramifications of any decision need to be considered, the notion of separate principles runs counter to a green approach. Inevitably principles will overlap. Nevertheless, the headings that follow are offered as a series of differing emphases among which a balance needs to be found for a green architecture to emerge.

Principle 1

Conserving energy

A building should be constructed
so as to minimize the need
for fossil fuels to run it.

St George's School, Wallasey, a pioneer ecological building where half the winter heating is provided by the warmth of the pupils in their classrooms

Past societies accepted the necessity of this principle without question. It is only with the recent proliferation of materials and technologies that such a basis for ordinary building has been lost. Whether by the use of materials or the disposition of building elements, buildings modified climate to suit the needs of the users. Moreover, the very idea of community comes from the sheltering of people together, whether to provide maximum areas of shade and cooler air between buildings or to reduce the external surface area of the community as it faced the hostile weather. People constructed their buildings together because of the mutual benefit to be obtained. A policy of cheap energy removed this generator of traditional community as surely as did the automobile.

Recent buildings that have attempted to reduce dependence on fossil fuels have tended to stand alone as separate experiments rather than cluster in patterns that respond to local climate. Consequently, such

experiments must be viewed as half-way attempts towards the creation of a green architecture. Many such experiments have also come from the committed individual rather than from the community as a whole, thereby further separating out the single achievement.

St George's School, Wallasey, Cheshire

An early pioneer of such an approach was Emslie Morgan who constructed a school at Wallasey, near Liverpool in England in 1961. Although designed to be solar heated through double-glazed windows, the school in fact achieved its significant energy conservation through high levels of insulation incorporated in the structure.[1] Some buildings are occupied by large numbers of people at a single time, some by very few. A school is a building intensively but intermittently occupied on both a seasonal and a daily basis.

To meet the problem of fluctuating heat demands the building at Wallasey combined a high level of insulation with considerable structural mass for thermal storage, so evening out temperature fluctuations within the building.

Since the war, schools in Britain have been designed to surround the children in their classrooms with natural daylight and sunlight. At Wallasey this approach was enhanced by giving each classroom a very large south-facing double-glazed window, with a wide (610 mm) separation between the vertical panes. Glare inside the building was reduced by the use of diffusing glass, with clear-glazed opening windows at intervals. Apart from the glazed wall, the building is constructed of insulated masonry. The 225 mm brick walls and 175 mm reinforced concrete roof are covered externally with 125 mm of expanded polystyrene insulation, itself covered with external cladding. The building is long and thin to obtain the maximum area of south-facing glass wall, and the roof slopes from the top of the solar wall down to the north side to reduce the volume to be heated. The building is also well sealed to reduce the infiltration of unheated air from outside.

It is significant that Wallasey was never intended as a demonstration of scientific principles; it was seen by the designer as a sensible and straightforward way of designing a school, and so it has performed for many years. Such ordinariness underlies the green approach to architecture. Nor did the building set out to be a demonstration of a novel approach to the development of form; it is rather the result of the concern of the designer with the performance of the building envelope. The technical problems of incorporating a large amount of insulation material into the fabric of the building will be known only to the designer and possibly to the contractor. The users might comment on the comfortable environment but they will be unaware of the skill that has been employed to create it.

In fact, at Wallasey the users unwittingly form an integral part of the heating system, together with the sun entering through the glass wall and the heat from the incandescent lights. As the floors and ceilings in the building are of concrete the building has a high thermal capacity, and this combined with the low ventilation rate keeps the surfaces of the building at a constant temperature. Changes in the external conditions take as much as a week before they are registered as changes within the classroom. In summer, if too much heat enters the building through the glass wall the temperature can be lowered by opening the windows. Thus control of the building is handed to the occupants. When the building is occupied the users put heat into store (in winter, in a normally occupied classroom, about half the heat input is provided by the pupils), and when it is unoccupied, the space remains warm until required. It is a symbiotic relationship: without the skill of the designers and the input of the users, the building could not function.

Dickleburgh Primary School, Norfolk

A more recent school built in pursuit of the conservation of natural energies is at Dickleburgh, near Norwich in England. In order to make use of the fact that the ground beneath is warmer than the air above in the winter months, the school needed to have its energy demand reduced through the use of high levels of fabric insulation. Then the energy balance could be made up from an electric heat pump system that draws on a supply of ground water in a chalk stratum beneath the site. The water maintains a temperature of 10–12 degrees C throughout the year. There

Dickleburgh Primary School, Norfolk, the heat pump system.
I Bore hole through clay/gravel, chalk/flint/gravel, and water-bearing chalk strata.
II Water pumped to two water-to-water heat pumps (III), and to the soakaway (IV). V Flow-and-return temperatures for the heating system.
Accommodation:
a sunspace; **b** classroom; **c** circulation/wcs; **d** kitchen/stores

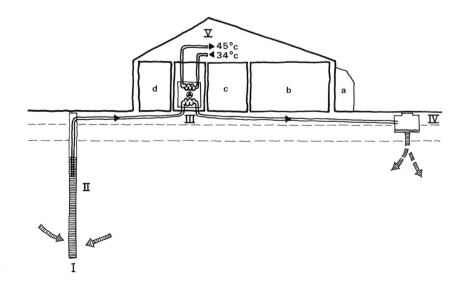

is no gas supply to the rural site, and the heat pumps, although run by electricity, enable electricity to be used more efficiently.

The elements of the school were arranged to maximize the energy potential of the site by placing the four classrooms facing south, creating a long elevation. The form of the single-storey building is approximately a triangle, with the narrow north elevation consisting of the kitchen stores and the plant room acting as a buffer for the shared accommodation at the centre of the school. The classrooms are covered with a further layer of climate modification in the shape of a pair of lean-to greenhouses used as conservatory spaces. These reduce heat loss and allow sun-warmed air to be drawn into the classrooms. After problems with overheating in summer the conservatories which originally ran the whole length of the south façade were modified to give each classroom a window into the conservatory and a window that ventilated direct to the outside.

The walls are formed of a single skin of brick and an inner skin of 140 mm polystyrene-insulated concrete blocks. The 100 mm cavity between the leaves of the cavity wall has 50 mm expanded polyurethane slabs attached to the inner surface (containing CFCs: the dangers of CFCs were not appreciated at the time of building), and the roof has a flat ceiling with 160 mm of mineral fibre between the joists. These measures give a good U-value of 0.25 w/m^{2}deg C for both elements (the U-value of a wall, ceiling or any building element is the measure of its ability to transmit heat, and hence depends on its thickness and the materials of which it is made). The south-facing windows are single glazed, while those facing north are double glazed. The building incorporates two heat recovery ventilation systems which extract air from the central core of rooms such as circulation spaces and toilets and feed preheated air to the activities hall. Overall, the building of 520 m^2 uses the following amounts of energy:[2] 'off peak' electricity (at a cheaper tariff) 8,700 kWh; 'on peak' electricity: 2,500 kWh. The use of off-peak electricity occurs because the heat pump is run at night for 80 per cent of the time. It is only run in the day-

time to top up the energy demand. For every 4.9 kW of electrical input to the heat pump, 17.4 kW of heat output is produced for the building by lowering the temperature of the ground water. While the overall efficiency of energy conversion is no greater than it would be were the fuel, whether coal, gas or oil, being burned directly to heat the building rather than first being converted into electricity, the heat pump system is a way of improving energy efficiency where, as here, there is no alternative to electricity for heating. The real energy savings come from insulating the building.

Dickleburgh Primary School, Norfolk, where the ground water heat pump system improves the efficiency of fuel conversion at a site where electricity is the only fuel available.
Architects: Norfolk County Council

Rocky Mountain Institute, Colorado

One of the most thorough designs for energy conservation is the headquarters of Rocky Mountain Institute, situated at Old Snowmass, in the cold climate of Colorado in the United States. At 2,165 m elevation, the winter temperature falls as low as minus 40 degrees C, and there can be weeks of cloudy weather. In spite of this, the building needs virtually no heating other than that provided by the occupants and the sun; two small wood stoves provide less than 1 per cent of normal heating needs. The key to this remarkable performance in such an extreme climate is superinsulation, with a wall U value of 0.14 W/m²K and a roof value of 0.09 W/m²K.

Walls are built of two leaves of 150 mm thick masonry, faced inside and out with local stone by a slipforming technique used by Frank Lloyd Wright. Between the masonry leaves is 100 mm of polyurethane foam (at the time of building in 1982, CFC-free foams were not available, but a special foam formulated to minimize CFC solubility and loss was chosen). The floor slab is reinforced concrete, with a skirt of insulation round the deep perimeter foundations to turn the whole floor into a thermal storage mass.

The roof is insulated to a high degree, and covered with earth to part-bury the building in its site. The weight of the earth necessitates a massive structure: 400 mm by 300 mm oak beams support 300 mm by 150 mm oak purlins which carry 75 mm-thick tongued-and-grooved cedar or fir decking to support the roof covering. To reduce the fossil fuel energy going into the structure, the wood was sawn to size at a sawmill powered by a wood-burning steam engine. On top of the decking are the usual polythene vapour barrier, more polyurethane, gravel, and up to 200 mm of soil and plants.

3

The windows in this unusual building are also special, using two panes of glass plus a further sheet of low-emissivity film between the two, to create the effect of triple glazing without the thickness. The cavities are filled with argon gas to reduce the heat transmission further, giving a performance quoted as twice that of triple glazing, and able to gain net winter heat even when facing north. Windows are concentrated on the south side to maximize solar gain, and this is increased by a 90 m² greenhouse set into the centre of the building, harbouring a large iguana under a fruiting banana palm. The mass of the masonry walls and the concrete floor, considerably over-designed to allow for a margin of safety, stores the heat for days when the sun is not shining. Ventilation

is provided by six air-to-air heat exchange units.

Hot water for the building is provided by a bank of solar collectors plus a superinsulated water storage tank holding about 7,000 litres. This allows all hot water to be provided by solar energy, and the propane-fired modulated-capacity instantaneous heater installed originally for back up is no longer used. To save water, Swedish wcs designed to flush with only 3–4 litres are used; the standard pattern of wc used in the United States needs about 20 litres, while the norm in Britain is 9 litres. Super-efficient nozzles are used for washing, saving both water and the energy needed to heat it.

The energy saving of Rocky Mountain Institute is not limited to the building fabric. Part

Rocky Mountain Institute, Colorado: the energy efficient kitchen. Even the cooker hood contains a heat-exchanger. Above right: the greenhouse provides solar heat for the building, but is also somewhere to grow bananas, and home to an iguana

of the building is an office, and this incorporates a low-energy computer and a photocopier that employs a cold process rather than a heated drum to set the toner that forms the image, reducing electricity demand by 90 per cent. A larger, hot fusion copier is designed and controlled to give 60–80 per cent savings. Nearly all lights are compact fluorescents of various types, and dimming controls take advantage of 95 per cent natural lighting. In the domestic part of the building a purpose-built fridge and freezer are much better insulated than normal models. The result is that the fridge uses about 92 per cent less electricity than an average conventional version, and the freezer reduces demand by 85 per cent. Clothes are dried on a passive drier, where solar heat is collected with argon-filled glazing and blown by small fans across the clothes hung on a rack below. Moist air is removed by a heat exchange unit. The only appliance not yet redesigned for energy efficiency is the cooker, which uses bottled pro-

pane gas, but a heat-trapping British kettle and double-walled Swiss pots save cooking energy.

The owner-builders, Hunter and Amory Lovins, estimate that their household electricity consumption is only about one tenth of the norm for their part of the United States, averaging 110–130 watts. They have also installed photovoltaic panels that provide two-fifths of the total electricity supply, including that to the 24-desk research centre, which uses about nine times as much electricity as all the lights and appliances. The extra cost involved in saving more than 99 per cent of the space and water heating, 90 per cent of the household electricity, and half of water use was paid back in ten months with 1984 technology.

R-2000 houses, Canada

Single buildings can demonstrate possibilities, but more significant energy savings become possible with a broader approach. Rather than producing communities of well-insulated houses, the R-2000[3] programme in Canada has trained some fifteen hundred builders to construct energy-saving family houses. These timber frame houses incorporate levels of energy saving that are appropriate for different locations in Canada. The masonry walls of the basement are insulated either on the inside surface or, preferably, externally, and insulation is also provided under the concrete basement floor-slab in some instances. The main walls of the house have two to three times the standard levels of insulation. To achieve this with stud wall construction, two separate stud walls are constructed with insulation placed in the outer stud wall, between the two walls and also in the inner stud wall. This method prevents cold bridging between the timber uprights (timber is not a good insulator when compared to conventional insulating materials). The polythene vapour barrier that prevents condensation in the structure and seals the house to prevent leakage of air can be placed on the outer face of the inner stud wall, two

Diagram of double stud construction to minimize cold bridging: **a** vapour barrier; **b** inner stud wall with insulation; **c** cavity filled with insulation; **d** outer stud wall

BELOW
Roof with raised heel truss, providing space to install a greater thickness of roof insulation

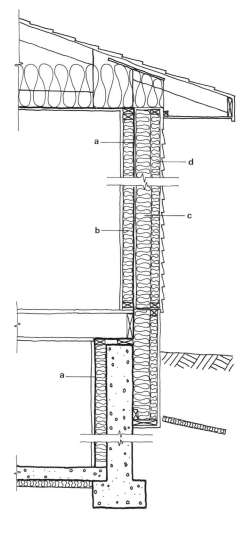

Exterior of R-2000 house, Canada

thirds of the way into the insulated structure from the outside. This means that it will not be punctured by the holes required for the installation of pipes and wires. The trussed rafter roof is constructed with a raised section that allows the installation of 200 mm of quilt insulation on top of the ceiling structure without interfering with roof ventilation at eaves level.

The other main energy conserving feature of the R-2000 houses is a heat recovery ventialtion system. Since the house is constructed to prevent all leakage of air into the warmed interior (by sealing the vapour barrier to the structure, and around all major openings such as windows) it is necessary to replace the natural draughts found in most houses with a controlled fresh air supply. The heat recovery ventilator passes the extracted air through a heat exchanger where the heat passes to the incoming fresh air, about 60–70 per cent of the heat being recovered in this way. Where fireplaces are included in the R-2000 houses they take the form of an enclosed stove or hearth with doors and a separate ducted air supply.

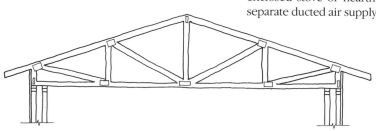

Another green feature of the R-2000 houses is the fact that they are made of renewable timber. Because of the natural forests and managed forestry industry of Canada there is a long tradition of building in timber there. Trees take carbon out of the atmosphere while they are growing, but when they are felled the carbon returns to the atmosphere whether the wood is burned or left to rot naturally. The use of timber in buildings helps to lock up carbon that would otherwise contribute to the excess that already exists in the atmosphere.

The R-2000 houses were originally produced as a response to concerns about the rising costs and falling availability of conventional fuels. The additional costs of the insulation were 'sold' to the house-buying public on the savings that would accrue from reduced fuel bills. This put such buildings firmly in the realm of the owner-occupier, and the architecture reflects this market. Mortgage companies have been prepared to allow a higher percentage of applicants' gross monthly income to count in the calculation of mortgage loan entitlement, in recognition of the lower monthly outlay on energy for the homeowner.

R-2000 house, Canada, detail of double stud construction

Low Energy House G, Hjortekaer, Denmark

The same technology of energy conservation is found in other parts of the world. A small timber house by the architect Bertel Udsen in Denmark was designed to save over 70 per cent of the energy needed to heat a similar but conventional Danish house.[4] The high levels of insulation meant that internal gains from the occupants – two adults and two large dogs, lights and appliances – provided more than 50 per cent of the heat needed. The house meets very high insulation standards with 200 mm of polystyrene insulation in the floor (U value 0.12 W/m²deg C), walls of two independent leaves with 200 mm of mineral wool between, and insulation also incorporated into the leaves (U value 0.12 W/m²deg C). The roof structure is formed of I-section hardboard and timber composite rafters at 1.2 metre centres, forming a 300 mm depth which is filled with mineral wool insulation (overall U value 0.09 W/m²deg C). The house was detailed to minimize cold

Draught lobby at the entrance to Low Energy House G, Hjortekaer, Denmark

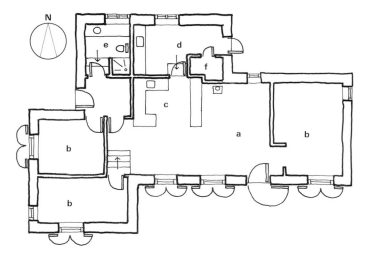

ABOVE
Plan of Low Energy House G, Hjortekaer: **a** living room; **b** bedroom; **c** kitchen; **d** utility room, **e** shower room/WC; **f** heating and heat recovery

FAR RIGHT
The dining area of Low Energy House G, simple and traditional in design, with wooden floor and ceiling. As with most green buildings, the inhabitants will be aware of the comfortable conditions but not of the methods and skills that went into achieving them

RIGHT
Insulation of roof, walls and floor of Low Energy house: **a** 300 mm insulation; **b** two 50 mm layers in plane of roof; **c** insulated shutters over windows; **d** 100 mm insulation in timber stud wall; **e** 200 mm insulation; **f** 75 mm perimeter insulation; **g** 200 mm insulation under floor

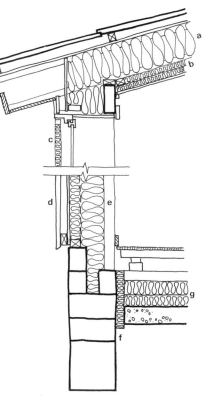

bridging at the junctions between wall and floor, wall and roof, and envelope and openings, and was designed to be as airtight as possible. A heat recovery ventilation system was fitted.

The living space within the house was organized around the south-facing façade so that use could be made of solar gain. The larger south- and west-facing windows are double glazed and have insulated shutters which can be closed at night (giving a U value of 0.52 W/m^{2}deg C, compared to 2.53 W/m^{2}deg C when the shutters are open). Elsewhere, windows are triple glazed and smaller in size. The south façade is provided with an overhang to the roof to give shade in summer. The windows can be opened for additional ventilation, and roller blinds on the inside can also be used to control solar gain. The house is very much under the control of the owners, with the modification of climate achieved through the use of shutters and blinds, the whole supplemented by a fast response heating system.

Externally the small, simple house is finished with stained timber boarding and the roof is covered with corrugated sheeting. The whole is reminiscent of the primitive hut, but here insulated to such a level that more than half the heating comes from the occupants.

Lou Souleu apartments, Avignon

Both the R-2000 houses and the Danish example represent responses to a climate of cold winters. However, the principle of conservation of energy resources applies also to warmer climates. At Avignon in France the climate is sunny throughout the year, with a rainfall average of 91 days per annum. The mistral blows across the area between February and April.[5] The apartment block named Lou Souleu, a public housing scheme, makes use of solar radiation but relies on the construction of the building to make the solar contribution significant. The block of twenty-two apartments is organized around a central glazed atrium which forms a common entry area. The apartments themselves are mainly

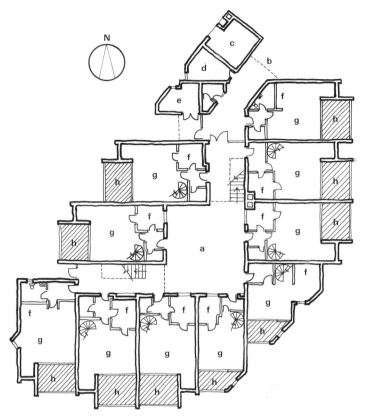

two storey, with attached two-storey conservatories, although there are smaller studio apartments on one level. The conservatories face to the south, the west or the east. A number of auxillary spaces such as the rubbish chute and stores are grouped on the north side of the block, and this, together with a reduction in window area on this side which receives the full force of the mistral, produces a marked contrast in elevations.

The block is constructed of reinforced concrete insulated with expanded polystyrene. The levels of insulation are not high (the roof has a U value of 0.43 W/m^{2}deg C, the floor 0.41 W/m^{2}deg C), reflecting the comparatively warm climate: the average ambient temperature in January is 3 degrees C. However, the disposition of the insulation allows the concrete of walls and floors, both ground and intermediate, to act as a heat store. The building is also constructed so as to be airtight, and a mechanical ventilation system is incorporated that draws air into the

Lou Souleu apartments, Avignon: **a** atrium, **b** entrance; **c** electrical substation; **d** bicycle/pushchair store; **e** rubbish chute; **f** kitchen; **g** living room; **h** sunspace. Architects: SCP D'Architectes Y. Contandriopoulos, C. Cimeray

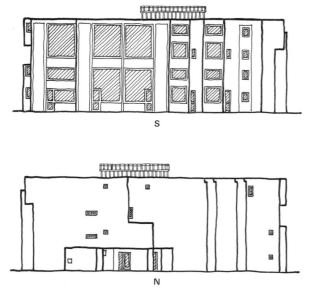

S

N

Lou Souleu apartments,
Agivnon, south and north
elevations. Below: the painted
sun near the entrance
reminds tenants that this is no
ordinary apartment block

produced an energy saving of 78 per cent for space heating for apartments facing south. When averaged for a south- and east-facing apartment, the saving was 67 per cent of the energy that would have been required to heat the same apartments built to conventional standards.

Some overheating of the sunspaces was experienced in the summer because the roofs of the conservatories could not be opened to allow stack-effect ventilation. The atrium also became very hot in summer, with recorded temperatures in excess of 27 degrees C. This was partly attributable to the failure of the mechanized blind system and the complexity of opening portions of the glazed roof to provide natural ventilation. As in many buildings of this type, what is simple and under the control of the residents, the insulation and the conservatories, works better than those elements that involve more complex technology that cannot be controlled easily.

The Lou Souleu apartments took the traditional methods of building such blocks and adapted rather than changed them. So with two further buildings, the first for a warm climate and the second for a much less sunny region.

building through the conservatories, so that the air supply is pre-warmed. In spring and autumn, as the conservatories become warm enough, doors and windows are opened between them and the apartments to allow the sun-warmed air to circulate. The block also has a solar water-heating system, the panels for which are mounted on the flat roof.

The measures taken at Lou Souleu have

Office and warehouse, Pecos, New Mexico

Monastery offices, Pecos, New Mexico. High-level clerestory glazing admits light and heat to the rear of the building

Architect: Mike Hansen

At Pecos, New Mexico, an office and warehouse building built for a publishing company run by the Benedictine Monastery looks largely traditional to the area. In form, the building is an elongated south-facing block with the warehouse space on the north side lit by south-facing clerestorey windows. The walls are of rendered and insulated concrete blocks (U value 0.47 W/m²deg C) and the roof has 150 mm of fibre glass insulation (U value 0.28 W/m²deg C).[6] The south-facing space is occupied by a series of offices, glazed and with heat storage provided internally by a series of water-filled drums under a bench behind the glazing. The heat is distributed inside the building through natural convection. Externally, insulated shutters can be used to cover the glazing during the cold, clear night to conserve the heat stored in the drums. During the day the shutters serve a second purpose as reflective surfaces to direct more sunlight into the building.

This simple technology is enough, in a climate that is sunny even when the air temperature is low, to give a building where the heating demand is so reduced that it is 95 per cent heated by the sun.

Doctors' surgery building, Sheffield

In a climate where the solar energy available in the heating season is not great the approach of conserving energy through high levels of insulation would appear more viable than attempts to design buildings to collect solar energy. One such building is a general practice surgery in Sheffield, England, that produces an 80 per cent reduction in the demand for energy for space heating although no new technology is used.[7] The construction and details are modifications to traditional UK masonry construction methods. The surgery is built of facing brickwork, a 150 mm cavity filled with resin-bonded glass fibre insulation and a concrete block

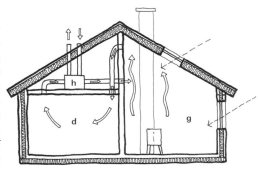

Heeley Green Surgery, Sheffield: **a** lobby; **b** reception; **c** office and records; **d** medical rooms; **e** treatment room; **f** store; **g** waiting area; **h** heat exchanger; **i** solid fuel stove. Solar energy enters through south-facing windows in the wall and roof. Stove-warmed air rises to the ceiling and is ducted into the medical rooms before passing out of the building via the heat exchanger, warming incoming air as it goes

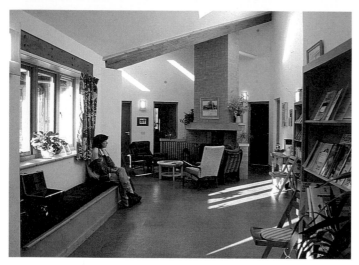

Heeley Green Surgery, Sheffield. Top: the roof and air supply; above: the sun-warmed waiting room. Architects: Brenda and Robert Vale

inner leaf (U value 0.2 W/m²deg C). The floor is a reinforced concrete slab (in order to span over existing rubble-filled cellars), insulated underneath with 150 mm of expanded polystyrene (U value 0.2 W/m²deg C). The roof is a conventional deep timber rafter roof (required because of the span) with glass fibre insulation between the rafters and an additional insulating sarking above (U value 0.1 W/m²deg C), covered externally with concrete tiles. The roof lights are standard factory produced triple-glazed units, and the windows in the walls are again factory produced, but are glazed with argon filled low-emissivity double-glazing units (U value 1.6 W/m²deg C). All windows are made of sustainable softwoods. The building was constructed with a

vapour barrier in the roof to be as airtight as possible, and a heat recovery ventilation system was installed to serve the whole building. In summer the windows can all be opened for additional ventilation.

Because the energy saving was achieved through alterations to the building fabric the form and appearance of the building were not determined by this requirement. The building is designed around a waiting room which faces south on to a garden, and while this disposition of space gives some incidental solar gain, it is used for the pleasure of sunlight in the waiting room rather than for the energy supplied. However, the mass of masonry in the insulated building, designed for both sound reduction and heat storage, gives an even internal temperature throughout the heating season. Additional heat is supplied from a solid fuel stove in the centre of the waiting room, which is also the centre of the building. Heat is distributed from this space to the rooms around the perimeter through the heat recovery ventilation system.

Casa Termicamente Optimizada, Portugal

Conservation of energy through high levels of insulation can produce a situation, as at Wallasey School, where no additional heating is required, all the heat being supplied by the occupants and from internal gains and solar gain through the windows. A project at Porto, Portugal, the Casa Termicamente Optimizada, was to produce a house based on common Portuguese construction that needed no additional fuel.[8] The site has an average minimum temperature in January of 4.7 degrees C and an average maximum in summer of 24.7 degrees C, although the temperature swings in summer, dropping on average by 11 degrees C, so that cross ventilation to cool buildings is a possibility.

The house is built using a precast concrete frame with an infilling of dense concrete blocks. The interior walls are constructed of the same material, 200 mm thick to produce a building with a high thermal mass. The exterior walls and the exterior faces of the columns are finished with 50 mm of expanded polystyrene and a sand and cement render. The same level of insulation, 50 mm, is used in the roof, and 25 mm of expanded polystyrene under the floor. Such levels of insulation, though low by standards of well-insulation construction in northern Europe, are sufficient to achieve the objective in the Portuguese climate, and resources are put into the building only as necessary.

Internally the accommodation is organized with the living areas and three bedrooms all facing south and service and circulation zones on the north side. Although the house fabric is used for storing and transferring solar energy, cylinders of water that stand like columns in the living room also store solar heat gains.

The main single-storey living area is placed four steps lower than the rest of the ground floor in order to increase the area of south-facing double glass in the bedrooms. Earth has been mounded up at the back of the house against the staircase zone, the staircase

and landing being lit by rooflights. The elevations demonstrate graphically the arrangement of the rooms within the house.

While the house produced satisfactory internal temperatures without additional heat, with an average indoor temperature of 15 degrees C in the coldest month of January, supplementary heat can be provided from a stove in the living room, in accordance with Portuguese custom. (Portugal does not have a tradition of central heating in houses.) The fireplace has its own source of ducted air, and the internal position of the chimney means that most heat from the stove finds its way into the house. Solar panels on the roof supplemented by an electric heater provide the hot water. In summer, cross ventilation can be effected by opening the windows on the north side of the house and one window on the side facing south.

The success of the house is achieved by the simple strategy of including as much insulation in the fabric of the building as is necessary to make the occupants and incidental

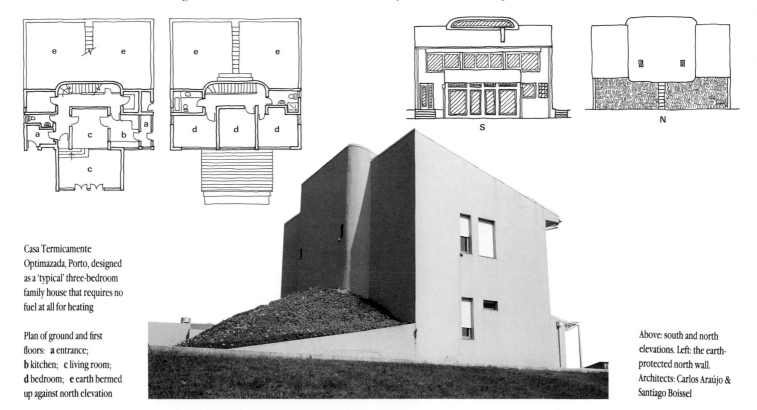

Casa Termicamente Optimazada, Porto, designed as a 'typical' three-bedroom family house that requires no fuel at all for heating

Plan of ground and first floors: **a** entrance; **b** kitchen; **c** living room; **d** bedroom; **e** earth bermed up against north elevation

Above: south and north elevations. Left: the earth-protected north wall. Architects: Carlos Araújo & Santiago Boissel

Living room of the Casa Termicamente Optimizada, Porto, with tiled floor and water-filled columns inside the glazing to provide the mass essential to store solar gains

tation of fossil fuels the main source of energy was wood. Firewood still provides about 15 per cent of the world's energy today. As wood became scarce, it seemed natural to many civilizations to make use of the heat of the sun to help reduce the need for wood to provide heat. The ancient Greeks were well aware of the benefits of solar design, and commonly arranged their houses to collect the rays of the winter sun. Greek cities such as Priene, following its relocation to avoid flooding, were laid out on a grid plan with streets running east-west to allow a southerly orientation of the buildings.[1]

The Romans continued the solar design principles that they learned from their contacts with Greek examples, but they were

gains into the major source of heat input. Levels of incidental gains from the sun and any required summer cooling can be enhanced by sensible organization of the spaces and opening windows within buildings. Neither of these measures is particularly costly, yet reductions of 75 per cent of the fuel that might be required can be achieved, and this in turn means a reduction of 75 per cent of the building's contribution towards the problem of carbon dioxide emission. Such obvious measures can and should form the starting point for any design project anywhere in the world.

Principle 2

Working with climate

Buildings should be designed
to work with climate and
natural energy sources.

The examples selected in the following discussion emphasize how building form and the disposition of building elements can alter internal comfort conditions, rather than demonstrating the reduction of fossil fuel demands through the use of insulation in the building fabric. Inevitably there will be some overlap in the two approaches.

In the days before the widespread exploi-

able to make use of window glazing, developed in the first century A D , to increase the heat that could be gained. Growing shortage of wood for fuel made the use of south-facing glazing popular for the villas of the wealthy, and for the public baths.[2]

The tradition of designing with climate to achieve comfort in buildings is not confined to the provision of warmth. In many climates the problem that faces the architect is to cool spaces in order to achieve comfortable conditions. The conventional modern solution, the provision of air conditioning systems, is no more than a crude process of opposing climate with energy, which was foolish when energy was cheap and pollution not considered, but is now verging on the insane.

Guest House, Dar-es-Salaam

Not all architects follow the conventional wisdom of calling in the services engineer to make their design work. In the design of a Guest House for Missionaries in Dar-es-Salaam, Tanzania, the Dutch architect Hubert-Jan Henket has used the building form and materials to modify the climate so as to produce comfortable conditions.[3] The site lies close to the equator in a hot-humid zone, and continuous air movement is a necessity if comfortable conditions are to be achieved. As Dar-es-Salaam is on the coast, diurnal land and sea breezes are available to provide this air movement. The design of the

Missionary Guest House at Dar-es-Salaam, close to the equator. Far left, looking up under the broad eaves; below, the white-painted roofs

RIGHT
Kempsey Museum and
Tourist Information Centre,
New South Wales. Light steel
cladding protects the walls,
and curved steel roofs shed
the sudden heavy rains

building exploits both these and the stack effect by which rising hot air within the building can be used to induce air movement.

The Guest House is planned as two wings of accommodation, each one room thick, and raised above ground level. The wings are connected at each end by the chapel and dining room, forming a central courtyard. The raising of the rooms and the hollow centre of the building allow free air movement, which is assisted in the rooms by large louvred windows. The roof of corrugated steel is painted off-white to reflect solar heat, and a ventilated cavity beneath it allows the stack effect to carry away the heat that is not reflected. The light colour of the roof alone reflects 55 per cent of the energy falling on it. Wide overhangs at the eaves shade the walls from solar gain, and a low mass structure ensures that heat is not stored to cause problems later in the day.

Kempsey Museum and Tourist Information Centre

The Guest House demonstrates a very simple approach to the design of a building that is to work in harmony with the natural environment, rather than against it. It co-operates with breezes and sunlight to create an internal climate that is more suited than the exter-

BELOW
Australian Aborigine shelters,
light strong structures
traditionally clad in bark

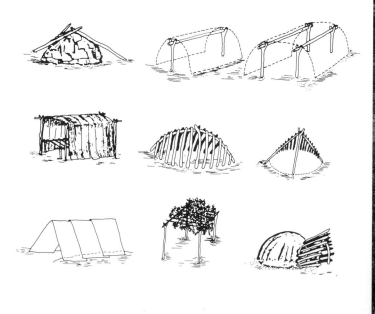

Kempsey Museum and
Tourist Centre. Plan:
a Museum; **b** Tourist
Information Centre; **c** small
theatre

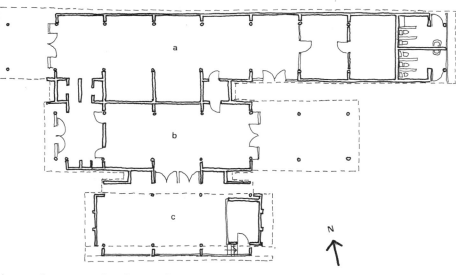

RESPONDING TO THE
SEASONS AND TIMES
OF DAY

RIGHT, ABOVE AND BELOW
12, 13 Variety of formal
expression is an essential
characteristic of green
architecture. Here the
response to climate is in the
hi-tech idiom. The Istituto
Tecnico Commerciale, a
technical school at
Montefiascone, Italy, built at
relatively low cost, uses
active and passive solar
technologies to reduce
energy demand by more than
50 per cent. On the south
façade, long windows are
covered with louvres that
adjust to the angle of the sun
at different times of day and
year. The vertical panels of
active solar collectors
between the windows feed
warm air to the heating ducts
inside the building.
Architects: IPR, srl, Viterbo

nal one to human comfort, but it achieves its aims using materials that are clearly non-natural. The same materials have been used by the Australian architect Glenn Murcutt for the Kempsey Museum and Tourist Information Centre, but in this building the architect is making analogies to the climate-modifying properties of trees. He sees the cladding of his building as comparable to the bark of a tree, protecting the interior from extremes of climate. The Australian Aborigines favour corrugated steel over all other modern building materials because it is very similar in its properties of strength and flexibility to the bark of which they traditionally constructed their shelters. It also has in common with bark the quality of lightness that is important to them.[4]

In the Kempsey Museum the exterior cladding of corrugated steel is fixed to a masonry wall, with 75 mm mineral wool insulation between. The masonry acts as a cool mass in summer and a warm mass in winter, while the steel and insulation 'bark' protect it from the extremes of climate.

The plan of the building, which houses the museum collection, a small theatre and the tourist information office, consists of three linear pavilions, with narrow linking blocks containing sanitary accommodation. The three pavilions are arranged with their long axes running approximately east-west, giving good exposure to the northern sun.

The climate is such that the building needs cooling in summer and warming in winter, and it must also cope with sudden heavy rain. The sun is allowed in to heat and light the interior by the simple device of angled louvres which cover the roof glazing that extends the length of each pavilion at the eaves.

The louvres admit the low winter sun to warm the brick mass, but they exclude the higher angled radiation in summer when the heat is not wanted, admitting filtered light like the leaves of a tree.

Kempsey Museum. Curved
roofs suggest an analogy with
the canopy of a tree

14–16 Another school, the Ecole Primaire de Tournai, Belgium, is designed with generous sunspaces to encourage pupils to respond to the natural environment. Classrooms and their small attached sunspaces are grouped round the hub of a large, double-height sunspace housing the library. On sunny days, as soon as the air is warm enough, the dividing doors are opened, and the small sunspaces are used for a variety of activities such as nature-study

Windows open from classrooms on to the central conservatory, giving light and ventilation. On the coldest days, only the classrooms are occupied

The entire building, like the kitchen (right), is alive with patterns of light and shade, constantly changing.
Architect: Prof. Jean Wilfart

FAR LEFT, AND INSET
17,18 Apartments, Les Garennes, in the new town of Saint-Quentin-en-Yvelines, France. Individual sunspaces punctuate the façade with cascades of glass, providing heating for the living rooms as well as a light and flexible living space. A north façade (inset) has a buffer row of shops along the street-edge, enhancing the advantage of apartments over single houses, in having fewer external walls through which heat can be lost.
Architects: L. Bouat, Y. Draussin, J. Guillaume, J. Massip

LEFT
19 An atrium in the PHICO Group corporate headquarters building, Pennsylvania, brings daylight in and adds to the open, airy character of the building without increasing the exposed perimeter-wall area. The large brick-built offices in rural Pennsylvania have minimal glazing on the barn-like north elevation, but three atria and plentiful southward-facing windows.
Architects: Metcalf & Associates with Keyes Condon Florence

CENTRE AND INSET
20–22 A broad glazed street
runs through the centre of
Niels Torp's SAS headquarters
building near Stockholm,
enhancing natural lighting
and modifying climate. The
users also gain from informal
meetings as they pass along
the street to use the shops
and cafés, restaurant and
swimming pool. The
designer's aim, to foster good
communications among the
fifteen hundred or so
employees, has led him to
subdivide the offices into five
distinctive buildings, each
with flexible, multi-purpose
meeting-spaces and linking
walkways at all levels

23–4 Even the designers of multi-storey buildings have responded to the green challenge. The ten-storey high Orbassano apartment block, Turin, illustrates active and passive technologies applied to a point block. Forty apartments face south-east or south-west on two wings. All open on to sunspaces that cover the entire height and width. The centre panel facing due south is composed of active solar collectors for warm air heating and hot water. Inset: a close-up of the glazing at one of the points of the building.
Architects: R. Gabetti & A. Isola

In the hot season a double-skin roof like that on the Guest House in Dar-es-Salaam uses the sun's heat to drive stack effect cooling, and large roof ventilators (which can be shut off as desired) allow hot air to escape from the interior spaces. The temperature of the brick walls drops, and because they are protected from the heat of the sun during the day, they remain cool. The Kempsey Museum's large rainwater gutters and downpipes are expressed clearly on the outside, making an architectural statement from the way the building interacts with its climate.

Internally the structure is very lightweight in appearance, with slender steel curved trusses supported on light tubular columns at 4 metre centres. The ceiling, like the roof, is of corrugated steel, curved to give additional rigidity (just as the bark roofs of Aboriginal structures are curved). Steel purlins spanning between the trusses support the roof on their top surface and the ceiling on their underside. The curving of the steel, part of the analogy to the spreading canopy of a tree, reduces the number of structural supports needed because the curve adds to the stiffness of the sheets, just as on a smaller scale the corrugations stiffen the flat steel sheet. The architect is working with climate and with an understanding of materials to create a building that is not profligate in its use of resources.

The Mary Flagler Cary Arboretum, Millbrook, New York

Glenn Murcutt's building makes an analogy with a tree in the way it modifies climate; the Cary Arboretum building owes its very existence to trees. It was designed by architect Malcolm Wells and engineers Dubin-Bloome Associates for the New York Botanical Gardens, and serves as offices, library, display and meeting areas and plant science laboratories. The plant science building, completed in 1978, was located in Millbrook, New York, where the climate gives cold snowy winters and hot summers.[5]

In appearance the building was aggressively solar; the form being dominated by the

need, in this cold climate, to maximize energy collection. The roof was arranged in a 'saw-tooth' profile like an old fashioned factory, but what would be north-facing windows in a factory were south-facing solar collectors on the plant science building. The collectors were angled at sixty degrees to the horizontal for efficient collection in winter. The north-facing roof slopes, with a pitch of thirty degrees, were covered with white shingles to reflect additonal energy on to the collectors, which were arranged in seven rows, each 33 metres long. The total collector area was 1,695 m^2, or two thirds of the floor area of 2,550 m^2.

Two different types of collector were used: one type consisted of steel panels with a selective coating to improve energy absorption and a double glass cover. These made up four of the seven arrays. The remaining three arrays had tubular collectors, each made of a 50 mm-diameter glass tube, with a silvered surface covering half the circumference. Inside this tube was a second glass tube, acting as double glazing, and inside this again was the copper collector pipe with its selective coating. The silvered coating on the outer glass reflected sunlight on to the blackened copper tube to heat the collecting fluid, a mixture of water and anti-freeze, which was circulated through both sets of collectors. The hot fluid passed through a heat exchanger where it heated water which was stored in two large concrete tanks buried under the building. One tank contained 19 m^3 of water, the other held 38 m^3. Heat could be put into one tank while heat was extracted from the other through the use of a heat pump running on off-peak electricity.

As befits a building where trees are studied, a considerable quantity of structural timber was used in the plant science building. The large beams supporting the roofs and solar collectors gave a sense of solidity and an appropriate reference to the forest. Walls were of 300 mm thick concrete with externally applied polystyrene insulation 90 mm thick and an outer coating of cement render, to give an adequate U value of 0.35 W/m^{2}K. The windows were small, double glazed, and covered at night with insulated shutters con-

Cary Arboretum, Millbrook, New York. The roof of the plant science building in its original form with ranked solar collectors

taining 25 mm polyurethane insulation. (Here again, the problem of CFCs in insulating materials was not apparent in the 1970s when the building was designed.) A heat recovery ventilating installation was used.

The plant science building was designed to obtain about 85 per cent of its space heating from the sun, an impressive performance in a climate where the winters are long and cold. It offered a very clear expression of the influence of winter energy collection on building form (though it could be said that if more insulation had been used, the collector area need not have been so large). Unfortunately the solar heating system proved too successful, and following excessive summer temperatures was replaced with gas fired central heating.

The Arboretum as initially designed makes an interesting comparison in terms of form with the buildings designed for hotter climates, where the roof serves as a shield from the elements. Shapes for energy collection and shade from the sun are both found within the form of the tree. However, whereas architects have blindly imitated the curved forms of Glenn Murcutt for buildings in very different climates that then needed to be made habitable through fossil energy use, few designers have emulated the energy-collecting properties of the tree, or studied the underlying meanings in climatic and cultural terms of the forms they borrow.

Istituto Tecnico Commerciale, Montefiascone

A third building that makes an analogy to the tree is the Istituto Tecnico Commerciale in Montefiascone, Italy, built in 1982 as a technical high school for commercial studies. Here, however, the architectural vocabulary is that of the modern factory or office building.[6] Louvres applied to the windows are the element of design that supplies the analogy. The construction is of load bearing concrete cross walls incorporating 70 mm mineral fibre insulation. These run north-south and form the basic structure of the six accommodation blocks, each three storeys high. On the north side the cladding is of insulated metal panels, each 1 metre wide and 10 metres high. The panels contain 60 mm thick foamed polyurethane, and are fixed to the outer edges of the concrete floors to avoid the possibility of cold bridges. The panels contain relatively small double-glazed windows. The ground floor and the flat roof are both insulated with aerated clay panels.

On the south side, the elevations are composed of insulated panels like those used on the north face, but in front of them are fixed solar air-heaters which cover 66 per cent of the south elevation. The remainder of this elevation is glazed, and these windows have internally adjustable sunscreening louvres

12,13

fitted externally, preventing overheating but allowing the users control over sun penetration and glare. The solar heating panels are connected into the warm air heating system for the classrooms, and consist of single glazing in front of black-painted corrugated steel sheet. The gap between the back of the sheet and the cladding panels has an adjustable air inlet at the base and feeds into the warm air heating ducts at the top. The solar radiation warms the steel sheet and heats the air, which is drawn up through the gap by fans. The insulated panels ensure that excessive heat is not transmitted to the interior. The solar heated air then passes to the classrooms via the heating system, and is supplemented as required by heat from a gas-oil boiler. The brightly painted ducts of the warm air heating and mechanical ventilation systems are a strong visual element in the interior. A bank of conventional solar collectors on the separate sports hall provides hot water.

The appearance of the school, like a tree, changes with the seasons. In summer the louvres on south-facing windows are almost closed to cut out glare and excessive solar heat, filtering the light like leaves. In winter the louvres are open to allow the low-angled winter sun to penetrate as far as possible into the classrooms, inviting the warmth like bare branches. The users are in control of these adjustments, and they also control the opening and closing of the windows to increase or reduce ventilation.

At the centre of the school is a large, three-storey-high conservatory which is linked to the top lit corridor that runs east-west linking the teaching spaces. The principal entrance to the building is via a dramatic steel bridge which penetrates the conservatory at first-floor-level across an open air arena. The image of the building is unashamedly technological.

The insulated construction gives the school an energy demand that is only 49 per cent of what it would have been had the construction been conventional. The climate is cold enough for heating to be required for much of the winter, with a January average temperature of 6.5 degrees C, and 2,190 degree days (base 19 degrees C). Of the total space heating requirement, 28 per cent is met by solar gains from the glazing and the air heaters, with a further 41 per cent coming from internal gains, leaving only 31 per cent of the load to be taken by fossil fuels. Since the demand has already been halved by the energy conservation measures, this is quite an effective performance.

13

Istituto Tecnico Commerciale, Montefiascone. North wall of small windows and insulated cladding panels. Protruding sections contain various services

Ecole Primaire de Tournai, Belgium

14–16

Possibly because they serve the generation that will inherit what is left of the planet, schools seem a popular building type for architects wishing to design with climate. At a school in Tournai, Belgium,[7] the low energy design is part of a strategy by the Belgian Ministry of Education to help to make pupils more environmentally aware. Large parts of the school have no auxiliary heating apart from solar gains, and the children use them only if the weather is appropriate. In summer they spill out into an open air theatre area and a garden, and in the middle of winter they retire into the classrooms.

The plan of the school is compact, with the classrooms round a large central conservatory on to which they have double-glazed low emissivity windows. Smaller conservatories are built off the ground-floor classrooms round the edges of the building. On the north side windows are small, while the south is a cascade of glass. The building is on four levels, with a semi-basement containing a multi-purpose hall. Being sunk into the ground improves the insulation. Walls and roof are fairly well insulated, with U values of 0.36 and 0.19 W/m²K respectively. The heat loss is 57 per cent of what it would be for a normally constructed school.

School heating is from two systems: 143 m² of air-heating active solar collectors supply

heat to a 49 m³ store filled with rocks in the east wing and a 4 m³ water store in the west wing. Monitoring of the building has shown that the water store is not very successful, largely owing to the heat losses incurred as heat exchangers take heat from air to water and back to air for the warm air heating system. The rock bed has been more effective, but it is not large enought to do more than pre-heat the east wing for two autumn months. The operation of the electric fans associated with the transfer of heat from the solar collectors means that the energy savings are not as great as was hoped.

The systems that work well at the school in Tournai are the simple ones. The central conservatory in which the library is situated is one of the areas that is not heated, except by the sun and by heat spilling from the surrounding classrooms. In winter, doors are opened into the conservatory on sunny days to allow the solar heat to warm the classrooms. In summer, vents are opened in the conservatory roof to allow the stack effect to extract unwanted heat and create a through-draught. These are simple technologies that

Ecole Primaire de Tournai: **a** entrance; **b** sunspace; **c** classroom; **d** library; **e** team room. The layout is in marked contrast to the conventional school plan of a row of classrooms entered via a corridor

The Ecole Primaire de Tournai. Interior of the great central sunspace, unheated throughout the year except by the pupils and the sun

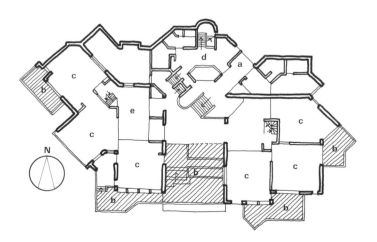

can be controlled by the users, and they need no fossil fuel energy for their operation. The most interesting lesson to be drawn from the school at Tournai is the idea of the building changing its uses of space according to the seasons, rather than opposing climate with energy.

Most of the examples described above are buildings set on individual sites. If a green approach to architecture is to have any meaning for much of the world, designers will have to tackle the problem of creating green buildings in the dense urban environments in which so many people live. Cities of necessity make multiple use of land both below and above ground for dwellings, shops, offices and transporation systems. To be relevant, a green architecture must respond to the need for multi-level buildings.

Apartments, Les Garennes, Saint-Quentin-en-Yvelines

Where the existing infrastructure within the town or city permits, the south-facing aspect of the street can be used to provide partial solar heating to multi-level dwellings. This is demonstrated by apartments on the Boulevard Ludwig van Beethoven in the new town of Saint-Quentin-en-Yvelines, near Paris.[8] The block is five storeys in height, with shops, day nursery and crêche on the ground floor. As well as being quite well insulated and constructed with double-glazed windows, the block has been planned with 70 per cent of its

17–18

Les Garennes apartments, Saint-Quentin-en-Yvelines. North elevation. The need to minimize glazed area on the north façade has not inhibited the variety of window-shapes

total window area on the south side, giving light and heat to living rooms and bedrooms. Conservatories are built over many of the windows to provide additional space and heat collection. The result is that 33.5 per cent of the space heating for a four-roomed apartment comes from solar energy, with a further 15.5 per cent from internal heat gains, leaving only half the load to be carried by fossil fuels.

The saving in heating comes from the manipulation of the fabric and the manipulation of the conservatory. The apartments use conventional French construction technology: the block has a reinforced concrete frame with structural partition walls 160 mm thick. The south-facing façade is made of *in situ* concrete between the members of the frame, again 160 mm thick, but with 80–90 mm of polyurethane insulation (containing CFCs) applied internally. The north-facing walls are similarly insulated, but are made of prefabricated concrete panels. Both the roof and the

intermediate floors are also of 160 mm reinforced concrete, with 60 mm of insulation applied. Although the insulation thickness is above the norm, wall and roof U values are only 0.4 W/m²K, and the internal placing of the insulation means that only the concrete floor and the internal partitions can act as a heat store. However, the limited area of external wall within an apartment means that the loss of thermal storage is less severe than it would be for a house of similar construction. The conservatories are fitted with shading blinds and opening windows. In winter the blinds are kept open and a simple fan operates to bring in the solar heated air from the conservatory to the living space. In summer the blinds are closed and the windows opened to prevent the build up of unwanted heat.

Les Garennes apartments, Saint-Quentin-en-Yvelines. South elevation with energy-saving sunspaces. Only half the space heating demand remains to be carried by fossil fuels

Orbassano apartments, Turin

The apartments at Saint-Quentin-en-Yvelines provide a street edge with shops without hindrance to a green approach. The problem comes in providing a block of suitable character on the north-facing side of the street. Here the planning must respond to the different orientation. No such problem occurs when housing is isolated in a point block, rather than given a street frontage. At Turin in Italy a similar response to high-rise living in the provision of conservatories or sunspaces attached to the apartments has produced a point block of strong form, with a good energy-saving potential.[9] The block is called Orbassano, and contains forty dwellings.

23–4

The triangular plan form of the block, while allowing all apartments to have an attached sunspace, has produced some rooms within the block which are rather deep and lit only from one end. The main access stair and lift lobbies are situated on the north wall and some apartments have bedrooms which are lit only by north-facing windows. The drama of the triangular tower block is enhanced by the contrast between the glazed southerly façades and the north wall, which with its repetitive arrangement of small square windows set without detail in the rendered insulated wall echoes the stylistic preoccupations of the so-called Rationalist architects in Italy. Here the Rationalism (if such it is) is relegated to the north façade where energy is lost rather than gained and rooms are only for use at night, while the 'living' side of the building interacts with the climate around it. A green architecture can only exist where designers and users share the overriding belief that working with nature is the only truly rational form of design.

The tower block at Turin, constructed with an *in situ* concrete frame, uses the solid concrete floor slabs to provide heat storage within the apartments. The south façades are clad with insulated steel panels incorporating windows with opening sashes. The conservatories thus formed heat up during the day, and the apartments can be opened into these

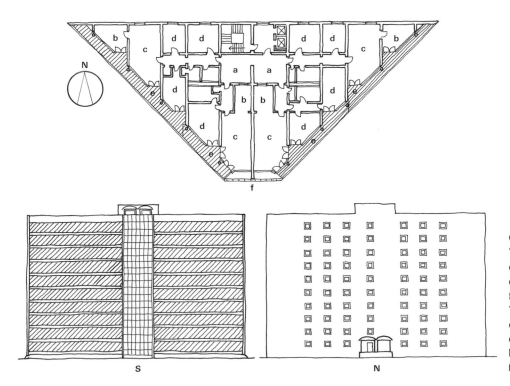

Orbassano apartments, Turin: **a** landing; **b** kitchen; **c** living/dining room; **d** bedroom; **e** sunspace; **f** solar hot air collectors. The south and north elevations (left) provide a dramatic visual contrast. Only bedrooms and entrance lobby face the rear

sunspaces by opening the double-glazed doors. Adjustable blinds allow the users to insulate the sunspaces on winter nights, and to control overheating to some extent in the summer.

These passive measures are augmented by a centralized active heating system which uses a south-facing bank of solar collectors to preheat the air supplied to the apartments from a mechanical ventilation system. The solar heated air is mixed with recirculated air, and additional heat if required is supplied by fan coils in the apartments run from a central gas fired boiler. The heated air from the solar collectors is also used to preheat the domestic hot water, which is raised to its final temperature by an electric immersion heater in each apartment. The block of apartments is constructed to a better standard than normal, so that its space heating needs in primary energy terms are only half what they would be for a building of conventional construction. The passive solar system provides 30 per cent of the space heating, with the active solar collectors giving an additional 6 per cent. The solar collectors also contribute 43 per cent of the energy needed for domestic hot water.

Orbassano apartments: the great energy-collecting wall, with opening windows and coloured panels. Below: an apartment door open on to the sunspace

Eastleigh Hostel, Hampshire

A different strategy for co-operating with climate is seen in two designs which create an artificial climate within which the building can operate. The first is a hostel for handicapped people designed by the Hampshire, England, County Architect's Department under Colin Stansfield-Smith.[10] This building consists of a number of flats and bed-sitters to allow people with various handicaps to live in the community but receive support to help them to cope with everyday problems. The accommodation is arranged in two rows along an internal street with planting and sitting areas. The whole building is enclosed by a steel framed glazed roof which creates a microclimate for the flats beneath it like a huge greenhouse, allowing the residents to use the spaces outside their flats far more often than they could were spaces out-of-doors. The umbrella-like roof acts as a symbol of the care offered by the building, but it is a care that is more than symbolic, since the roof is also acting as a modifier of climate, enabling the users to experience the weather without being out in it. The presence of the roof makes the construction of rooms and flats beneath it simpler than if they were outside, since they need no elaborate waterproofing.

Eastleigh Hostel, Hampshire, a small-scale development of flats and bedsitters for handicapped people, under a sheltering roof

Headquarters building
for Scandinavian Airlines, Stockholm

20–2 A similar approach can be seen in the Scandinavian Airlines headquarters in Stockholm, Sweden, designed by Niels Torp.[11] This is a very large office building, purpose built for the user as is typical in much of Europe and Scandinavia. The chief executive of the company wanted a building that would break down conventional office hierarchies to allow chance meetings and the opportunity for creative developments to spring from them. The architect's response has been to design the building round a broad glazed street, full of cafés, restaurants, trees, waterfalls and bridges. As people pass between the offices, or use the sauna, swimming pool and other facilities, they meet in the street which

links all the spaces. As well as being a meeting space, the glazed street is a collector of solar energy and a modifier of climate, helping to reduce the energy costs of the building. It also allows greater use of natural light in the office spaces, which has a significant impact on overall energy demand.

The buildings described show differing responses to the need to work with climate and natural resources, and if none is a fully 'green' building, in all of them the designers have attempted to co-operate with the natural environment rather than design in conflict with it. They also display a very wide range of formal responses in this attempted co-operation. There is no one style that must be used, but a variety as broad as the fauna and flora of the earth which have evolved to suit the particular conditions in which they live.

BELOW, AND RIGHT
SAS Headquarters building, near Stockholm, general view. Each of the five buildings fronting the indoor street has a different formal quality. Right, a flat roof makes a sun terrace under the massive glazing

Principle 3

Minimizing new resources

A building should be designed
so as to minimize the use of new
resources and, at the end
of its useful life, to form the resources
for other architecture.

Although this principle, like the others discussed, is directed towards new buildings, it acknowledges that immense resources are already a part of the existing built environment, and that the rehabilitation and upgrading of the existing building stock for minimal environmental impact is as important, if not more so, than the creation of a new green architecture. There are not sufficient resources in the world for the built environment to be reconstructed anew for each generation. Nor would it be right that it should be so, unless the layers of history that each generation applies to the built environment are to be ignored. So much of what is admired about buildings comes from associations, and an objective assessment of a building with no prior knowledge of its purpose or ownership is virtually impossible. Even a demolished building leaves traces, such as an entry point into the site, that need to be respected by anything new put in its place.

Re-use can take the form of recycling materials or recycling spaces. The recycling of both buildings and building components is part of the history of architecture. St Albans Abbey, for example, which was rebuilt between 1077 and 1115 on the site of a Benedictine Abbey, used Roman bricks taken from the ruins of Verulanium at the bottom of the hill to reinforce the walls of flint, the only building stone available in Hertfordshire. The prefabrication methods of later medieval timber frame buildings whereby the pieces were cut and fitted together in the carpenters' yard, marked, disassembled and moved to site, meant that portions of medieval buildings could be moved if required, and even now often turn up in unexpected places. Sometimes whole structures have been moved to find a new purpose.[1]

Often those whose access to resources is least have demonstrated the way in which structures designed for one purpose can be adapted to suit a different need. However, the alterations necessary can often more or less obliterate the original form of the structure or building. This produces a dilemma for those concerned with the conservation of buildings that has to be acknowledged. Should a building be preserved unchanged because it was once important, or should it, because it can still be made useful, be conserved in a changed state? A green approach to the problem might suggest that the question be decided on resources alone. If the resources required to alter a building are less than for demolition and rebuilding then the

former course is adopted. This, however, fails to acknowledge the historical importance of the structure, which might suggest that other values need to be considered. This dimension to the problem of changing existing buildings to make them meet present needs, especially in terms of upgrading buildings to improve thermal performance which may alter appearance, can be summarized as the paradox of Venice. If global warming produces even a small alteration in sea levels the future of Venice is again imperilled However, if steps are taken to reduce the energy used in buildings, then the same buildings may have to change in appearance. To preserve Venice, it may be necessary to conserve buildings in an altered state. It is important that these

issues now form part of the debate of building conservation.

Some extraordinary schemes have been created through the re-use of large redundant buildings even without thought to thermal performance, such as the Gare d'Orsay in Paris, which is now the Museum of the Nineteenth Century. The difficulty of inserting a series of spaces to illustrate nineteenth century paintings and sculpture in a vast volume that was intended to accommodate the then-new electric trains poses architectural problems which are, perhaps, not necessarily happily resolved in this instance. However, the benefits accruing from re-using a large piece of the urban fabric that has a presence in the city can override the internal considerations. The refurbishment of existing housing areas in cities and towns can also offer a considerable saving in resources over demolition and rebuilding, and avoid disruption of the community.

Green architecture is about the adaptation of old structures as well as the creation of new ones. The Gare d'Orsay in Paris is an example of the recycling of an important urban structure after it has ceased to serve its first purpose. Built in the nineteenth century to accommodate the then-new electric trains, it was first re-used as a car park and now houses the Museum of the Nineteenth Century. Conversion: Gae Aulenti

Apartment blocks, Berlin

In Berlin, the wall which formerly severed west from east also broke through a pattern of high density housing related to the centre of the city. Some of this housing found itself in West Berlin, separated from its centre. The area of Kreuzberg consisted of high density city blocks made up of four or five storeys of apartments built over shops around the perimeter, with a mixture of further apartments, workshops and small factories grouped around inner courts in a largely unsuccessul attempt to bring light into this dense centre. It was housing typical of any European industrialized city, surviving into the post-industrial decades. For most of the twentieth century the intention had been to clear the area and rebuild. When Hardt-Waltherr Haemer became director of Altbau[2] this policy was reversed.

To avoid disruption of the community, existing empty buildings were refurbished first to provide space for residents while their own homes were being renovated. The blocks were first made structurally sound,

Run-down inner city apartments, Kreuzberg, Berlin, have been upgraded to keep the community they housed intact. One block has been designed as an ecological conversion with solar energy systems, water economy, and waste water filtered through the roots of plants (the common reed, in other contexts a plant used for thatching). Where flats have been demolished the spaces are planted

weathertight, and insulated. Further improvements, such as new kitchens and bathrooms, and the rearrangement of space to remove those apartments which were very small, were only undertaken in consultation with the tenants. Self-help refurbishment was encouraged, and standards of heating in the rehabilitated apartments were such that the tenants would still be able to afford to pay the fuel bills. The strategy of refurbishment of the dense urban blocks had energy benefits, since the apartments have relatively few external surfaces from which to lose heat.

The dense mix, however, also meant that the apartments in the centres of the block lit from internal courts remained dark. In an effort to overcome this, some of the courts have been planted, and some of the smallest enlarged.

The policy of conserving the existing housing fabric and doing only what was most needful to improve the lives of the residents has been successful in keeping a community together: 95 per cent of those affected by the rehabilitation programme have remained in the area, and of these, 61 per cent are still in their original apartments.[3]

RIGHT
Brandram's Wharf, London: a warehouse before and after conversion into flats. Top: the shell; right: the entry courtyard

Brandram's Wharf, London

Redundant buildings that were never designed for human occupation can be adapted to provide housing for a community. The masonry and external frame structures of Victorian warehousing, for example, provide the kind of spaces that can be sub-divided for many different uses. The housing schemes in London's Docklands depend upon such flexibility. In one such scheme, a co-operative that owns the warehouse, together with the architects, have provided flats at low rents for single people, with a frontage to the river.

Brandram's Wharf is in the main a brick warehouse with a cast-iron frame whose timber floors had been gutted by fire, although part of the building had a concrete frame and concrete floors. The existing space was divided into twenty-four two-person, six three-person and four four-person dwellings, all entered from a courtyard carved from the original building and open to the sky. The flats are designed to be shared, although each single person has his or her own room.

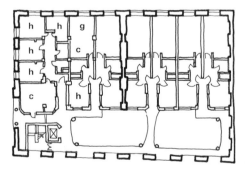

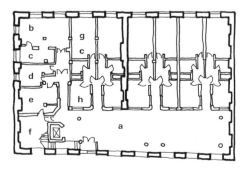

Ground and first floor plans:
a entry courtyard;
b meeting room;
c kitchen; **d** laundry;
e plant room; **f** dustbins;
g living room;
h bedroom. The first floor (above) is divided into six two-person flats and one four-person flat

Although the energy of the tenants has been involved through the co-operative who own and manage the housing, the apartments are not particularly energy conserving. This raises the issue of the way money was apportioned in the job. Although an example of the useful retention and re-use of a building, and thereby part of a green approach to design, at Brandram's Wharf money was spent on reinstating lost brickwork details (required because the building was listed as of historic interest) in preference to measures to minimize energy demand.[4] This shifts the Venice paradox to London. If sea levels rise, the Thames will rise. Because of the inability of those who commission, use and design buildings to accept their responsibility for global warming, this riverside conversion may have no long-term future.

Other conversion schemes work with site and climate to produce an architecture that is respectful and also looks to the future. A barn conversion in Suffolk, England, has made use of the two-storey opening in the south-facing elevation to introduce thermal collection and control. The existing fabric of the barn has been repaired and insulated internally. Living spaces are placed behind the opening, which has been glazed in. The original barn doors have been retained, and now form external insulated shutters which can be closed over the glazing at night, partially opened in overcast weather to admit daylight as required, or fully opened in sunny weather to maximize solar gain. The old skin of the building is responding to climate as surely as any other vernacular building in the area.

Materials and parts of buildings that have outlived their usefulness *in situ* also have value, a value that forms the basis of a thriving architectural salvage business. Again, it is necessary to consider the energy involved in this recycling to ensure that overall, the resource-use of new or existing parts in the building is minimized. The fact that a designer has used a scrapyard technology is no guarantee of a building designed to conserve resources. The Bohemia Jazz Club in Japan, for example, is filled with scrap from the air transport business, with old aircraft seats, repaired and recovered, placed below a re-creation of an aircraft wing hung with discarded aircraft engines, all highly polished and carefully selected to give the former rubbish the status of expensive architectural decoration.[5] Similarly, a material that was developed after the war to make use of rubble at a time when traditional materials were in short supply has found a place in an expensive housing scheme. The wartime material was a cyclopean concrete that used pieces of brick and stone rubble as the aggregate. At a house in Sussex designed by John Outram for a Swedish industrialist, the 'red-marble' pre-cast columns are formed from a type of so-called 'blitz-crete', for which selected new bricks are distributed in a mould by hand before the concrete is poured in. Once set, the surface of the material is ground in a process similar to that for terrazzo and polished to expose the selected aggregate surface.[6] Thus a material originally intended to be cheap in resources is made expensive. It is a long way from the squatter settlements which make use of the waste materials of the rich.

25 Exterior of Brandram's Wharf, London, the conversion of a disused Victorian warehouse building into co-operative riverside flats. The robust detailing retains the spirit of the old building.
Architect: Levitt Bernstein Associates

Architect Nigel Coates' design for the Bohemia Jazz Club, Tokyo, where patrons occupy refurbished aircraft seats. Energy saving is so far incidental to fashion, but benefits in some cases may be real

THE NATURAL HOUSE

26–9 Awareness of a range of indoor pollutants – radon, formaldehyde gas, carcinogenic wood-finishes – has turned designers' attention to the need for healthy buildings, non-hazardous to builders and users alike. The Murphey residence, hidden among trees on a private island off the Atlantic coast of the United States, is built and furnished with natural materials whenever possible. Tropical wood from controlled timbering areas is finished with non-toxic products such as linseed or citrus oils. Natural fabrics are chosen in preference to synthetics

RIGHT
A deck of untreated timber is planned around an existing tree, uniting the built and natural environments

FAR RIGHT
A wooden spiral staircase winds towards the light in a tower like a growing tree. Heat-recovery ventilation and a ground-water heat pump for warmth and cooling are two of the strategies adopted to save energy and avoid pollution

User Participation

30–3 The requirement that a building shall remain relevant and functional for as long as possible is an important consideration for green architecture. One way to achieve longevity and avoid demolition is to design buildings that are capable of adapting to the users' changing needs. At the Open School, Belfort, Belgium, basic forms are as varied as the materials and colours chosen. A deliberate lack of uniformity within the overall plan invites the users to make their own modifications as need arises during the life of the building.
Architect: Lucien Kroll

34–7 Terraced houses at
Graz-Puntigam, Austria (left)
and apartments at Graz-
Algersdorf (right and inset)
were designed by architect
Eilfried Huth in consultation
with the families who would
live in them. The result is
considerable variety within a
regular framework. All the
dwellings were designed for
their particular occupants,
but the very fact of such
variety means they can be
adapted by present or future
owners without detriment to
the plan

THE USER AS BUILDER

LEFT, AND INSET
38–9 A self-built house hidden in the English countryside makes use of local materials. Here the architect David Lea specified saplings cut during tree-thinning, and specially grown straw as wall-filling and for the roof. The owner and her friends constructed the small house almost entirely with their own labour

An English stone barn attached to the house, adapted as living space with a full-height glazed opening and massive doors as insulating shutters. The barn interior behind has been converted into a galleried hall with tile flooring, and the lower part of the glazing slides back to give a clear view of the garden. All the oak and elm timbers used in the conversion were second-hand.
Architect: David Clarke Associates

Houses at Hornby Island, Vancouver

Elsewhere, designers have exploited waste materials provided by both human beings and nature. At Hornby Island, near Vancouver, a former carpenter, Lloyd House, has constructed a series of houses that use the driftwood washed up on the island's beach. Driftwood is just one stage in the cycle of timber growth and decay, whatever force first put the wood in the sea. Since the wood is worn smooth, warps and splits as a result of its time in the water, House sees these visual qualities as signs of the history of the timber, and each piece of driftwood is studied in order to relate its history to the most suitable place in the new dwelling. The houses are not drawn, and decisions about the placing of certain bits of timber and elements such as doors and windows are made as the construction of the house proceeds. The waste timber is not used to give shape to an intellectual idea about space, but the spaces are allowed to grow out of the quality of the available material. As House himself stated:

The experience of building should be a joy. If it isn't in the construction, you can't expect to feel it in the finished building. A building should act as a touchstone, and as a source of nourishment.[7]

Such building is obviously more possible on an island without any building legislation to constrain structural ideas. However, just as the respect for the waste material of driftwood gives character to the houses, so respect for waste influences other areas of the islanders' lives. The island has a depot where unwanted products are brought to be sent to the mainland for recycling; organic waste is composted, and to save water, houses have composting lavatories. There is also a free store where items no longer needed by one islander can be left for the next. If the interest in recycling now being manifested in Western societies brings with it anything like the respect for materials that is found among the builders and designers of Hornby Island, a very different architecture may be the result, with materials again forming the starting point for architectural design. The society that espouses conservation of resources and recycling of waste materials may well find that William Morris's dictum, that one should

Houses on Hornby Island, Vancouver, built of waste material, timber reclaimed from the sea. The houses are unique, reflecting the individuality of the architect-designer and the owner, as well as the particular wood available at the time of building

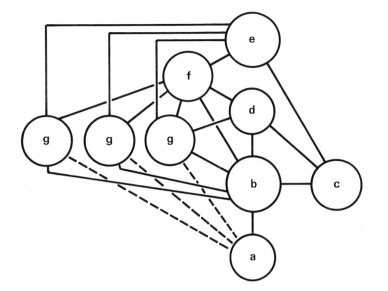

Bubble diagram for a small office building, mapping optimum arrangement of the spaces (anti-clockwise): **a** lobby; **b** reception; **c** waiting room; **d** interview room; **e** conference room; **f** kitchen; **g** offices

do nothing to a material except that which honours it best, has much to offer.

One honour to be given a material is to try to ensure that it can be re-used at the end of its first life. From the point of view of the designer, there are two paths by which to follow this idea. The first involves the technical expedient of using materials that can be recycled and systems of construction that can be dismantled without destruction. The second, perhaps more sophisticated approach is to recognize that certain dispositions of spaces can accommodate a wide variety of human activities; that space itself can be multifunctional.

Without entering into the argument about what constitutes 'functionalism', one aspect of its influence on architecture has been the design of spaces specifically to house named activities. In the 'bubble diagram' beloved of design students the relationships between a whole series of named activities are examined in order to discover the optimal physical arrangement of the activities, an arrangement which can then be translated into the physical spaces of the building. In other fields, this logic has produced diagrams which optimize the layout of kitchens, with the famous work triangle that embodies the order in which kitchen work is to be undertaken. Such specificity runs counter to any possible optimization of the space by the user. A 'green' approach to the design of a space for cooking might be to conceive of a multi-functional

space where cooking can take place, but in an order so far as possible dictated by the user. The space might also be used as a playroom, a place for conversation, a place for eating, a place for reading. What is necessary is that there shall be sufficient space allowed for such additional activities.

A variety of building types have lent themselves to multifunctionality. The form of the English Georgian terraced house, for example, has proved highly adaptable and has at various times been converted into flats, offices, shops and even a school of architecture. The building is essentially a load bearing masonry construction with rooms of such a size that many different activities can be housed within them, all accessed off a central circulation zone or staircase.

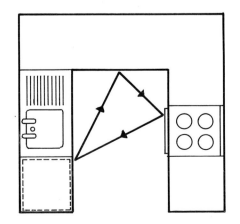

The so-called 'work triangle' of efficient kitchen layout

Centraal Beheer, Apeldoorn. Structural grid with circulation grid overlaid, showing the spaces created at intersections (shaded square, right)

BELOW
The various ways in which the spaces may be arranged: three-person office; meeting room; washroom/WC; sitting area: refreshment room; two-person office

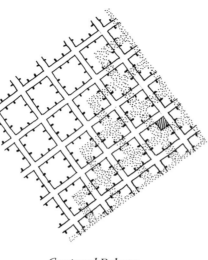

Centraal Beheer, Apeldoorn

More recently, Herman Hertzberger in the Netherlands has attempted to design for multiple use of space in new buildings. The office building of Centraal Beheer in Apeldoorn, built for an insurance company, provides an architectural structure within which office spaces can be organized by the users. The building is ordered into four quadrants of working spaces, separated by a core which holds elements of circulation and social space, including internal public streets:

Mother with her children may walk in to meet father: they may have a drink together or, as many families do, lunch together in the restaurant. This openness is intended to break down conventional barriers between work and home, public and private, building and street.[8]

In essence, the building has a structural zone of split columns which define where circulation takes place. At some points this zone of space between the split columns is taken vertically through the building to allow light into the centre. In turn, the circulation zones define discrete spaces which can become variously work areas for differing numbers of people from one to four, or contain lavatories, meeting spaces, restaurant areas, etc. Services are carried in the ceiling which is articulated to accommodate them, the articulation reflecting the circulation grid. The ordered fragmenting of internal space is reflected in the exterior of the building and in the number of entrances into the internal streets.

Although Centraal Beheer is an office building it provides space that can have different uses within this context, and an interaction between what is public and what is private that allows the distinction between work and home to be blurred. The energy of

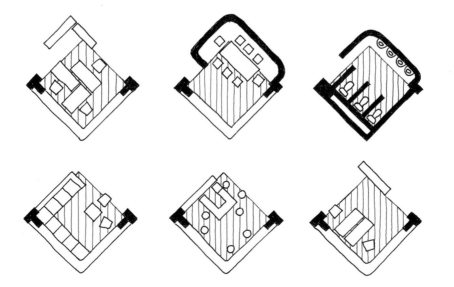

RIGHT
Interior of Centraal Beheer, the first office building to attempt to reconcile the needs of the organization with the demand for individual identity. Employees are encouraged to peersonalize their workspaces

Centraal Beheer, Apeldoorn. The exterior reflects the division of the interior into small units

the users is given a chance to determine the spaces in which they are to work. The architecture has been withdrawn to the point of providing a structured environment in which some individuality is possible, and a structured environment that can accommodate future change.

Apartments, Copenhagen

In other circumstances, multifunctional spaces can be incorporated during the upgrading of buildings. The conservatory, for example, is a space which not only modifies climate but, according to the weather and the inclination of the users, can become a sitting space, dining space, greenhouse, or place for the display of plants. In the rehabilitation of a block of apartments in Copenhagen, Denmark, a new wall of conservatories was used both to reduce energy demands and to provide additional living spaces.

The new glass façade is supported by columns of larch wood, and the floor has a cavity through which fresh ventilation air passes before entering the conservatory. The air is thereby heated a little, which reduces condensation on the inside of the glass. The conservatories are only single glazed, since

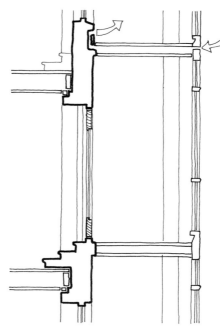

LEFT
Baggesensgade apartments, Copenhagen, section through sunspace to show the height of the floor in relation to the living room, and the airflow through the sunspace floor

the apartments already had double-glazed windows and the occupants were concerned that multiple layers of glass would cut down both the light and the feeling of proximity to the outside.[9] To ensure further that sufficient light enters the apartment below, the floor of the new conservatory is fixed 450 mm above the level of the apartment floor. To allow a view out from the apartments the conservatories are, therefore, glazed from floor to ceiling.

In fact, during the first season of use very little energy was saved by the conservatories. It was found that the occupants were leaving the doors from the apartments into the conservatories open, even on days when no appreciable solar gain had warmed the glazed spaces. During the second heating season savings of 34 per cent in energy consumption compared to that before the refurbishment were achieved; the occupants were using the system with more care. Savings resulted from the reduced heat loss from the building through the buffering effect of the conservatories and through direct gains on sunny days when temperatures were high enough to open the doors and windows between the apartments and the conservatories. Such evidence emphasizes the relationship between the users and a green architecture. A build-

ing, whether new or recycled, is no longer an object designed and provided by an expert to be consumed by a non-expert. A green architecture of necessity involves the occupant in its use, even in something as simple as opening a door to a conservatory once the temperature inside the glazed space is higher than that inside the building.

A conservatory is just one example of a space that has many functions and can contain many activities. If the approach of multi-functionality is applied more widely it will allow buildings to adapt to changing needs. Compared to the modern industrial shed, the mill buildings of the nineteenth century with their traditional materials can be repaired and put to new uses with ease. Increasingly, it is the older buildings that are rehabilitated and recycled and the modern buildings that are demolished to become only so much rubble, in a world that can ill afford such wastefulness.

It was the co-operative tenants of Baggesensgade apartments, Copenhagen, who decided that their older, inner city apartment block should be upgraded with a wall of new conservatories, rather than merely renovated. Window frames of different sizes were preferred for visual interest, and larchwood support columns were chosen to introduce a natural element. The new conservatories added welcome space to the small apartments, especially as the tenants found them warm enough to sit in during three-quarters of the year. Architect: F. Stein

Principle 4
Respect for users

A green architecture recognizes
the importance of all the people
involved with it.

This principle may appear to have little relevance to issues of pollution, global warming and the destruction of the ozone layer, but a green approach to architecture that includes respect for all the resources that contribute to making a building will not exclude human beings. All buildings are made by hand, but in some architectures this fact is acknowledged and appreciated, whereas others have attempted to deny the human dimension of the building process. Only in Japan have robots been developed to take over some of the human roles on building projects, but for a robot to work effectively the project-scale must be such that the same task, or a limited series of related tasks, can be repeated many times. At a very different scale, the small builder still has to rely on personal skill for a number of unrelated tasks, drawing on expert subcontractors where there is no alternative.

A greater respect for human needs and labour can be evidenced in two separate ways. For the professional builder, it is essential that the materials and processes that form the building are as little polluting and dangerous to the individual worker or user as they are to the planet. Architects have begun to realize the extent of the global or human poisons that may be found on building sites, and that it is no longer feasible to use insulating materials that contain CFCs, or to use methods of timber treatment that are carcinogenic. Alternative methods of detailing to protect timber physically become preferable to the chemical approach. Perhaps were designers to regard timber as living wood, as in the vernacular tradition, rather than as some squared and dimensionally stable material, the temptation to cover everything with chemicals might be lessened.

ABOVE RIGHT
In Germany, a family house with a number of energy saving features, including a double sunspace, was constructed mainly by the owner and his family over a period of three years. The main structure is concrete post and brick construction, with internal and external timber cladding. The Waldmohr Solar house, Landstuhl, is part of a low energy housing project funded by the German Ministry for Research and Technology. The trees surrounding the house filter light in summer, but allow sunlight to enter in winter, after the leaves fall. Architect: Prof. Thomas Herzog

The Masters Corporation

In the United States, an architect, Paul Bierman-Lytle, has founded a building company based on the old principle of the 'master builder', when architect and builder were one and the same person. One of the aims of this company is to offer clients buildings that are free of the toxic materials that form such a large part of the environment in which many people are forced to live and work. In a recent project for a 500 m² house on a 15 hectare island off the Atlantic coast of the United States, materials known to be hazardous have been avoided studiously. The list of products that are excluded includes synthetic wallpapers, solvent-based adhesives, plywoods and chipboards containing formaldehyde, and fitted carpets which can harbour the dust mites that cause allergic reactions in susceptible people. Decoration of the house uses natural fabrics rather than synthetics, and timbers only from sustainable sources. It is slightly ironic that the owners of the house, a direct-marketing consultant and stockbroker, use an aeroplane to reach their non-toxic home, but the techniques involved are not applica-

26–9

ble only to the very rich. The use of materials and finishes made of natural products rather than synthetic chemicals can be applied to any building, and Paul Bierman-Lytle is setting up a shop to sell non-toxic paint, linoleum (made from linseed oil, it is a natural alternative to vinyl flooring) and similar products not easily available from conventional suppliers. The aim is to produce buildings that are less of a health hazard for those who inhabit them and those who build them. In fact, Paul Bierman-Lytle became interested in this field because he began to feel ill with coughs and sneezes when he was working as a builder.

Environmental Defense Fund headquarters, New York City

The same techniques can be applied to the conversion of existing buildings. In a design for the Environmental Defense Fund, a non-

profit-making advocacy group, the architect William McDonough took care to specify materials and finishes that would be healthy for the people using the building, a conversion of an existing office space. The architect spent some time helping the clients find a suitable building. He then designed a layout using daylight wherever possible, and incorporating natural materials such as stone desktops and beeswax-finished wood floors. Colour balanced triphosphor lighting and high ceilings give an outdoor feel. The New York ventilation code is based on volume of space, not on the number of occupants, and high rooms, ironically, mean a higher rate per person than needful. This again, raises the dilemma of balancing benefits and energy penalties. More ventilation may well lead to higher energy consumption because of the need to heat so much fresh air, so that the users will have a healthy working environment, but will inhabit a wider world made increasingly less tolerable through the polluting effects of fossil fuel consumption.

A self-built home

The other form of human involvement that needs to be considered is the positive involvement of the users in the design and construction process. If this energy remains uninvolved, a resource is being wasted which could inform the finished product and extend its usefulness. A range of buildings, some built by the owners, some involving large groups of people, have made use of this resource and the result has been a high level of satisfaction with the buildings created.

A small, largely self-built house, hidden in the English countryside, made use of the labour of the owner and friends while also attempting to use locally available materials in a resource-conscious way. The cottage designed by architect David Lea is constructed of small-diameter saplings cut from a wood as part of the process of thinning. The saplings are formed into arches, stabilized longitudinally by the battens for the thatch and the oval form of the building. Furthermore, the building is designed to meet the

38–9

Interior of Environmental Defense Fund office, New York city: interior of corridor known as 'the Boulevard' because of its evocation of the outdoors. Task lighting supplements daylight entering through windows to offices on the right. Natural materials and finishes of varying shades and textures are part of a strategy to provide a healthy and stimulating work environment

Eldonian community housing
project, Liverpool.
Architects: Wilkinson, Hindle,
Halsall, Lloyd Partnership

ground without the use of conventional
plastic waterproofing:

> ... apart from the hoop ends there are no
> foundations, only a clearing of the topsoil.
> The whole thing stands on a bed of gravel
> drained at the sides by a land drain and
> built up with hardcore at the lower end.
> The gravel board allows the inside gravel,
> topped with nothing more than a 50 mm
> sand/cement screed and carpet, to remain
> 200 mm higher than the outside.[1]

The walls have a filling of straw in the
lower parts, and are covered with render
inside and out. The roof is thatched with long
straw, no longer a waste product of agriculture but purposely grown for thatching. The
thatching was accomplished by the owner
herself after attending thatching lessons, as
was most of the building and its fittings, once
the structural frame had been erected with
the help of friends and the architect. The
small house with its single space is unique
and extremely individual to the owner who
constructed it. Here a number of green principles have been followed to produce an
architecture which, although undeniably
exclusive, is also instructive.

Communal inner city renewal project

In other circumstances the energy and enthusiasm of much larger groups of people have
been united to achieve a goal that affected
the built environment. Liverpool is a city
which had already seen major disruption to
the communities at its centre when major
road developments were forced through
after the war. The communities who lived in
the area of Vauxhall had seen work lost to
them as the docks declined. The area had
already once been redeveloped with walk-up
tenement flats in the 1930s. The new proposal was to clear these same flats and
rehouse the community across the city.
Headed by the local Catholic church, the
community opposed the demolition, until
someone on the council suggested the
inhabitants should organize themselves into
a housing co-operative, and 'the Eldonians'[2]
were formed.

The decision to take charge of their own
housing was perhaps the easiest step in the
whole process, for the relationships between
the city council pushing for its own version of
urban regeneration, the residents, their advisers and designers and the Government

housing agencies were complex and none too friendly.[3] Nevertheless, the final result has been houses with gardens on streets built in consultation with the people who were to live in them:

> The design time for 145 households participating fully in the detailed design of their houses for that site ... took thirty-two evening meetings over a period of eight months. Who said participation in design takes an inordinate length of time?[4]

The site on which the Eldonians were finally allowed to build became vacant when a factory which had formally given employment to some 1,700 people, many from the surrounding area, was closed. Such regeneration involved coping with inner city land which had become polluted over the years of industrial development: sulphates, phenols, cadmium and arsenic were found in the

ground. The reclamation of the community and the land offer a model of the possibility for change in derelict inner city areas. The energy of the local Eldonian community has even brought new work into the area through a business set up to produce wholesale plants and shrubs, and to provide skills for local landscape maintenance. The 'Garden Market', although a small beginning, demonstrates that housing regeneration can bring community-led and approved employment into an area.

Terraced housing, Graz-Puntigam

Whatever the considerable political achievements of the Eldonians, both the houses and the housing layout as built are conventional in form and materials; nor are the buildings any more energy efficient than other contemporary structures. However, elsewhere in

LEFT AND OVER PAGE
Terraced houses, Graz-Puntigam, Austria, designed by Eilfried Huth in consultation with the future occupants

Europe architects are balancing the formal demands of architecture with the users' needs to express their own views on design, with more interesting results. In the Austrian city of Graz, Eilfried Huth has produced some impressive participative housing. Huth has been described as:

> … that rare kind of architect who believes that people should be allowed to display their own taste in their houses rather than dominating them entirely with his own.[5]

The terraced housing at Graz-Puntigam which was built in the late 1970s shows variations in size, plan form, fenestration and colour that are expressions of the participation of each family involved in the project. However, the overall simplicity of layout, with the pedestrian access at either side of a central bank of planting, brings the individual houses into a whole: a whole that is further emphasized by the repeated roof formations. The structure provided by the designer has enabled each family to live in a purpose-designed house while remaining part of the group.

Apartments, Graz-Algersdorf

A further scheme of participative apartments at Graz-Algersdorf shows a much tighter overall organization because of the nature of the apartment housing type. Yet here, too, individual families were able to contribute to the design process, even to the extent of a top floor projection added at the last minute to provide space for the extra child of a particular family. The community participated in the

project before the architects were appointed, deciding that the three developments should each be given to a different designer. The block designed by Huth contains 26 apartments in a curved form which semi-encloses a garden; it meets the street in a stair-and-lift tower serving the central four-storey part of the development. The apartments vary in both size and the means by which they are accessed, and some are for the disabled. Within the overall framework the apartment plans also vary considerably, responding to the needs and wishes of the users. These differences find less expression on the façade than with the terrace housing, but the participation is nevertheless there, with the tenants being consulted on the overall plan and the development of the communal areas.

Apartments at Graz-Algersdorf, Austria, designed by Eilfried Huth, where the curved form of the block helps to create a sense of enclosure and community

37

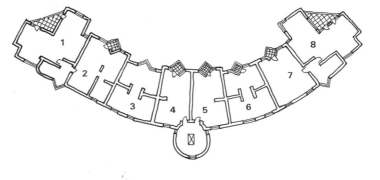

Apartments, Graz-Algersdorf. Plan showing the various shapes and sizes of apartment enclosed within the broadly symmetrical form

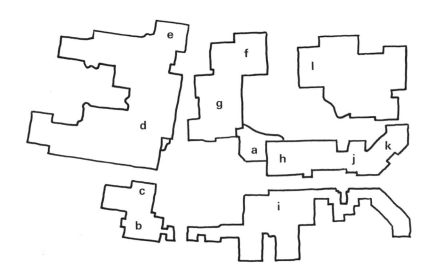

Layout of the Open School, Belfort: **a** pupils' social centre; **b** administration; **c** light engineering; **d** heavy engineering; **e** medical centre; **f** electronics; **g** general studies; **h** restaurant and kitchen; **i** dressmaking and fashion; **j** library; **k** information and registration; **l** gymnasium

*Open School,
Belfort*

Open School. Roof-shapes are as different as the activities carried on in the buildings under them

The energy of a community can find expression in buildings other than housing. The open school at Belfort, Belgium, by Lucien Kroll, a friend of Huth, involved the participation of the local administration, teachers and a local association working in social housing (as housing was to be included in the overall project). The open school follows Kroll's development of an architecture of variety. Kroll has claimed in his writings that uniformity can stifle individual expression. Where the doors of a street of houses are all painted the same colour, it will

take the courage of a maverick to paint one door differently. If, however, the doors are already different, then alterations to suit the user become much easier.[6]

The underlying structure of the Belfort scheme has been established by the architect. The open school is laid out like a village of buildings around a square, with the main entrances to the departments opening from this central space. The building section is changed to produce diversity, and the materials of the different buildings are many and varied. The heavy engineering department, for instance, is housed in a shed like a factory with metal cladding, whereas the drawing studios have a timber structure and are finished in warmer colours. The identity is produced by the architect, but within the framework comes the opportunity to alter the spaces to suit the user. Such is the complexity of the concept that it cannot ever be destroyed through alteration; it can only be enhanced.

What Kroll seeks to develop is an architecture which does not so much spring from the process of participation as encourage user-participation throughout the life of the building. This does no more than recognize the creative energies of people, energies that produced whole traditions of vernacular building before design theories were ever dreamed of.

Some architects have argued that the

30–3

energy of the users will never become assertive without the development of a new type of professional designer:

> The backbone of the process of production we envisage is a new kind of professional who takes responsibility for the functions which we now attribute to the contractor. He is responsible for the detailed design of the houses and for making sure that the actual design is in the hands of the family. The system of construction, which is the key to the possibility of his work, is under his control and is being continuously changed and improved by him. And he is responsible for the process of construction itself.
>
> He is, in a nutshell, a modern equivalent of the traditional master builder.[7]

Self-build systems

Christopher Alexander attempted to put such thinking into practice with the construction of a group of houses in north Mexico in 1976. Although grouped around a communal space, the houses were designed to suit each family's needs and budgets, and were largely constructed by the families themselves. Such activity follows the precedent of many poor families who build their own houses with what they can find because there is no alternative. What Alexander seeks to do is amplify this process so that the houses can be better built and serviced, and more closely matched to the family's needs, and yet still be affordable.

Such a process finds a mirror in the developed world with the work of Walter Segal and his development of a timber framed house type specifically for the self-builder that can adjust to meet the needs of the individual family. The Segal system used timber as the material with which most people are familiar and which can be worked with basic skills. The materials used were just sufficient for the purpose, with elements such as foundations reduced to basic post on pad, sparing of both labour and skill.

Open School, Belfort. Irregular design extends to asymmetrical windows

Systems of self-build and user participation now need to be reconciled with appropriate climate modification in order for a sustainable approach to design to be fully realized. Attempts have been made to take the Segal system of timber construction and make it more energy efficient, but systems of building based on machined timbers are still problematic in countries where most of the timber is imported. However, in other areas of the world the use of the vernacular way of self-help building has been married with vernacular traditions of climate modification in the effort to produce a sustainable architecture. Part of the stated aims of the Community-based Building Programme in Papua New Guinea could be taken as a model for this goal. They are, 'to develop and implement':

> (i) A form of architecture and building culturally, environmentally and economically appropriate to Papua New Guinea.
> (ii) Building and planning processes which enhance the opportunities for people to participate in the shaping of their own environment.
> (iii) The production and use of durable, aesthetic, local building materials.[8]

The buildings that have resulted from these aims in Papua New Guinea are traditional in making use of shaded outside areas, platforms for living raised clear of the ground, and cross ventilation provided through the roof form. However, the materials used are the most appropriate rather than purely traditional; for instance the roofs are covered in timber shakes rather than corrugated iron which, though commonly used, has poor heat-moderating properties. Although not a material traditionally found in Papua New Guinea, shakes are used on other Pacific Islands. Such a material can be pre-cut, as was most of the post and beam frame, so that the houses can be constructed by the owners with the help of one trained carpenter.

The Papua New Guinea example should not be too easily dismissed as inappropriate to the developed world. The industrialization of the Third World, with all this implies in increasing energy use and thermal and other pollutions, needs to be balanced by changes in the developed world. An architecture that modifies climate has in the past been an architecture that was constructed at least in part by the users. If a green architecture seeks to make maximum use of all the resources that are put into the built environment, then human energy and enthusiasm should not be left out. A green architecture should be able to make experts once again the servants of people's needs, rather than the masters.

HARMONY WITH
LANDSCAPE

40 A semi-buried house in Catalunya, Spain, harmonizes with its rocky site. Deep overhangs to the windows and an awning keep the house pleasantly cool in summer. Architect: F. Javier Barba

LEFT AND FAR LEFT
Traditional self-built houses: timber shakes and post and beam construction in Papua New Guinea

The Segal self-build house system, adapted by the Centre for Alternative Technology at Machynlleth, Wales, with softwood frame construction and such energy saving features as solar panels and composting wc

RESPECT FOR SITE

LEFT, ABOVE AND BELOW
41–2 Two buildings that
'touch-this-earth-lightly' – an
Australian Aboriginal saying
expressing respect for site.
Underground houses
designed by Donald Metz in
New Hampshire allow the site
to flow over them almost
undisturbed

RIGHT, ABOVE AND BELOW
43–4 Malcolm Wells chose to
bury his Cape Cod house
(above) along an earth-ridge,
collecting solar energy
through a line of roof-
windows rather than facing to
the south. The cross section
through his house at Raven
Rocks Ohio (below) shows
how a building can be buried
in a hillside, preserving
almost all the natural site, yet
still be flooded with sunshine

THE GREEN ROOF

45–6 Low-maintenance roof gardens. Planted roofs such as these literally preserve the site, raising it up and putting back into the environment some of the beneficial life that even a green building must remove

Principle 5
Respect for site

A building will 'touch-this-earth-lightly'

The Australian architect Glenn Murcutt quotes an Aboriginal saying, that 'One must touch-this-earth-lightly'.[1] This saying embodies an attitude to the interaction of a building and its site that is essential to a green approach, but it also implies wider concerns. A building that guzzles energy, creates pollution and alienates its users does not 'touch-this-earth-lightly'.

The most direct interpretation of the phrase to 'touch-this-earth-lightly' would be the idea that a building could be removed from its site and leave it in the condition it was before the building was placed there. This relationship to site is seen in the traditional dwellings of nomads, but their lightness of touch is not just a matter of moving their homes, it also concerns the materials with which they build, and the possessions they carry with them.[2] The black tent of the Bedouin is woven from the hair of their goats, sheep and camels. When erected, the tent cloth adopts a low, aerodynamically efficient profile to avoid damage by high winds; it is kept in place by long ropes, also woven from hair, and supported by a very few wooden poles, because wood is a scarce resource in the desert.

The Netsilik Inuit people of northern Canada carry their tents in the summer when they need to follow the game that are their food, but in the winter the skins that form the tent cover are dipped in water and wrapped round frozen fish. The long bundles freeze solid, and are joined in pairs with caribou bones. A mixture of moss and slush is rubbed in and allowed to freeze smooth to turn the tent skins and frozen fish into a sledge to carry the Inuit and their possessions over the snow. The parts of a nomadic structure must serve several functions, because only a minimum of possessions can be carried from place to place. Over generations the items necessary for survival, comfort and the continuation of culture have been determined.

While societies have abandoned the nomadic ife for one in fixed dwellings and architecture has come into being, there is still a continuing demand for temporary structures for exhibitions, performances and other cultural manifestations. These structures frequently take the form of tents; however, an interesting example using very different technology is the sculpture pavilion designed by the Dutch architects Benthem Crouwel for the Sonsbeek '86 festival.[3] This building was designed to protect fragile works of sculpture placed outside, and so the structure was intended to be almost invisible. It used only four materials: precast concrete for the footings, laminated glass for the walls and roof, steel for trusses and connections and silicone mastic to stick the panes of glass together. Fins of glass glued to the glass walls gave additional rigidity, and provided a place of attachment for the light steel trusses that carried the flat glass roof. The floor was the earth, merely covered with wood shavings to prevent it from becoming muddy. At the end of the event the building was unbolted and removed, the foundations were lifted and the soil replaced, the shavings were raked up, and the site was completely unaltered by the events that had taken place on it. The building could be taken away to be used elsewhere for another exhibition, or recycled into another structure.

Bedouin tents, a sophisticated response to site and resources

Quodropod house, Queensland

The sculpture pavilion is an obvious and self-explanatory example of lightness: it was so light visually as to be virtually invisible. A slightly different solution to site-disturbance is shown in the Quodropod house designed by Gabriel Poole.[4] Here the aim of the architect is to leave the site in the Queensland rainforest in an undisturbed state by inserting his building and allowing the natural world to flow under and around it. The house stands clear of the ground on slender steel posts braced with fine steel cables. Disturbance during construction is minimized because the structure needs no conventional footings. If excavating machinery were brought into the forest to dig the foundations, as for a conventional dwelling, it would cause considerable damage to the site. The damage would be exacerbated when narrow access roads were subject to heavy loadings, causing soil compaction over an area much greater than the site alone. A house built with the Quodropod system uses hand-dug foundations. The other materials – corrugated steel roofing sheets, timber, steel mesh and plastic or canvas screens – can be carried to the site by hand. Existing trees, usually felled by conventional builders, are accommodated by allowing them to continue growing through holes made in the deck and the roof where required. The finished building has a very lightweight appearance, and is open to the cooling winds. Living in it is as close as possible to living in the forest which surrounds the house on all sides. During bad weather, screens can be rolled down to cover open mesh panels in the walls. Despite, perhaps because of, its lightweight construction the house is designed to withstand cyclones: a case of bending like a reed rather than standing up to the blast like an oak.

The Quodropod house 'touches-this-earth-lightly' in a most literal sense, leaving the site undisturbed except by the few small pads that support the steel legs. This is a strategy that can work well in a hot climate where the building is required to be airy and open to the cooling flow of the breeze. In a cold climate a building has to provide enclosure, warmth and protection from the hostile elements. One way of achieving this while respecting the site is to unite the building positively with the earth on which it stands.

LEFT
A Quodropod house in Queensland, scarcely disturbing its forest site

Interior of a Quodropod house, open to cool breezes

Cottages, Leicestershire

One of the finest exponents of this approach was Ernest Gimson, working in Leicestershire in England at the beginning of the twentieth century. He built a series of cottages in the Charnwood Forest using the materials of the site as far as possible. One of the best-known examples was planned round a rock outcrop which was incorporated into the spatial planning and structure of the cottage. The rock became part of the chimney, and the fall

Ernest Gimson's Stoneywell Cottage, Leicestershire, incorporating a rock outcrop

of the users, Gimson's cottages display those qualities that are found in vernacular buildings. The difference is that Gimson's work is the conscious design of a highly competent architect, rather than the craft of a country builder. His success lies in the rigour with which he applied the principles of using local materials and responding to local conditions, without allowing his architectural knowledge to override these primary concerns. His skill is used to create simplicity. It is an irony that Gimson designed the cottages as weekend homes for businessmen who, as part of the whole industrial development process, were helping to destroy the vernacular architecture he was trying to recreate.

of the ground around it created a series of changes of level within the ground floor plan. Another Gimson cottage[5] is built of stones gathered from local fields. Gimson was concerned to roof the cottage with the local slates which are rough textured and multi-coloured, affording a good surface for the growth of the lichens that give the old roofs their characteristic appearance. At the time of construction quarries that produced the slates had ceased to be worked. Gimson's solution, to preserve the local character of his work and maintain its links to the site, was to use recycled slates from old buildings demolished locally. Pieces of slate left abandoned in the quarries when work ceased were also used as lintels and hearthstones, and as blocks in the walls. The use of such local materials and the siting of a cottage adjacent to a great outcrop of rock has a twofold effect. First, the house appears to grow without perceptible break from the ground on which is stands; it becomes in effect another outcrop of the natural landscape. Second, the cottages in general have an extraordinary timeless quality.

In their use of natural local materials and their unforced variety of plan forms, responding to the site conditions and the needs

Underground houses

An alternative to building a house of the materials of its site is to bury it in the site so that the ground can flow over it undisturbed. The recognized history of architecture covers only a brief part of the time that people have used the resources of the planet to provide themselves with shelter. For example, extensive use has been made of natural shelters, caves, or homes buried partly within the earth.[6] In the part of China known as the loess belt the soil consists of a soft silt that can be

Chinese underground houses grouped around courtyards. Standing figures at the top left indicate the scale

Architect's office, New Jersey, an early example of modern earth-sheltered architecture, built by Malcolm Wells

carved and excavated easily. Dwellings were dug out round sunken courtyards some 500 m² in area and 8–10 metres deep. The land above the houses can be used for farming. The courtyard allows light to enter the dwellings, but the solid earth surrounding the other sides of the excavation, combined with the deep layer of soil over the roof, means that the dwellings stay at a very constant temperature with little need for heating fuel.

Two underground houses in New Hampshire

The possibilities of building within the earth, to save energy and restore the landscape to its former appearance, have been explored in two houses in New Hampshire.[7] The houses, which were both designed by the architect Donald Metz, conserve energy by being buried in the earth and also collect energy by facing walls of glass towards the sun from the south. Both houses incorporate deep overhangs to the edge of the grass-covered roof to shade the glazing in summer but allow the low winter sun to penetrate. However, while the two buildings are similar in their

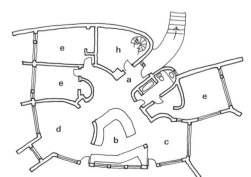

Plans of two underground houses by Donald Metz: Top, Winston house; below, Metz house: **a** entrance; **b** kitchen; **c** dining room; **d** living room; **e** bedroom; **f** music room; **g** study; **h** utility room/store; **i** garage

response to the local climate and topography, the architecture of each is very different, as is shown in the plans. The Winston house has a Miesian simplicity, with the living rooms, including the kitchen and study, buried in the hillside. The simplicity of the approach is reflected in the elevation, which enhances the landscape by contrasting with it.

41

42   The Metz house follows more closely the contours of the hill and curves around to provide parallel bands of living space within the shell. Externally, however, the white-painted buttress walls do not belong to the hillside in the same way as the simple stone retaining walls that flank the area beneath the living space. The choice of finish is foreign to the natural materials on the hillside, but the resulting contrast is not carried through into the form of the building itself.

A green architecture as natural as, for example, the underground houses of the Chinese belongs to its place. An architecture that works with nature but remains under the control of intellect can produce a worthwhile contrast, as is shown in the first underground house, while an architecture that imitates nature without respecting all its aspects of place and climate may be formally less successful.

Buried house at Catalunya

A similar project in Spain[8] is sited on a hillside facing south with views to the Mediterranean, two kilometres distant. The site is 2,000 m² in area, and the house itself has a floor area of 220 m², but because the whole house is set into the slope of the site and the house roof is covered with turf, the site area is not diminished. The structure is concrete to resist the pressure of the soil on the walls and to carry the weight of the 300–600 mm-thick earth-layer that allows grass to grow on the

40

South elevation of the Winston house, New Hampshire. Deciduous trees have been planted where they will shade the glazing in summer

roof. The great mass of the structure and the effect of the earth that surrounds it combine to give the building a high thermal mass and allow it to remain cool in the summer without need for air conditioning. Winter heating is not a great problem in the Mediterranean climate, but the house is better insulated that the norm, to reduce its heating needs. The green effect is spoiled by the use of electric heating, a disaster in primary energy terms.

People with the means to commission a weekend house with three bedrooms, two bathrooms and a floor area of 220 m² could presumably have built any form of house they chose, and the fact that the house at Catalunya was designed in accordance with some of the concepts of green architecture may be seen as encouraging.

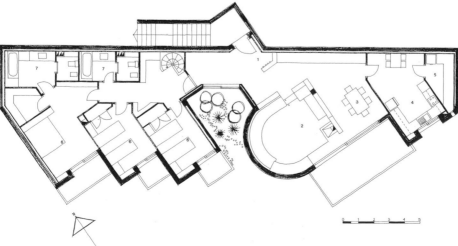

RIGHT AND FAR RIGHT Semi-buried house, Llavaneres, at Maresme in Catalunya. The living room faces southwards towards the sea, with curved windows (see plan). A tiled floor stores solar warmth. A view of the entrance (far right) shows how the grass-covered roof blends with the garden

The planted roof

Section through a planted roof, indicating the measures needed to retain moisture to allow the plants to grow, to provide insulation, and prevent moisture entering the building

system is complex to avoid problems. Any roof type needs the following layers:

1 Vapour barrier bonded to roof deck.
2 Insulation: this must be able to withstand water and the pressure of the soil.
3 Waterproofing and vapour equalization layer.
4 Root barrier and second waterproof layer; if roots are not stopped by a positive barrier they may grown down and penetrate the waterproofing.
5 Separation layer to allow relative movement between the planted layer and the waterproofing below.
6 Protection layer to prevent damage to the layers below.
7 Drainage or water-retention system; if the roof retains too much water the plants will suffer root damage, if it drains too freely they will die by drying out: the choice of system

A less extreme variant of the idea of burying the building in the earth as part of a strategy for restoring the site is to build a conventional building and cover the roof with vegetation. In this way there is no loss of planting area, and in addition, areas of greenery can be provided in cities where there were no plants before by the use of such roofs on new buildings. The depth of soil that can be provided on a roof is not great because of the loading involved. To provide sufficient soil to permit a normal range of plants to be grown necessitates a structure of unusual strength to carry the weight of the soil, the problem being worsened when the soil is full of water.

Mindful of the attraction of the green roof, at least one European roofing materials manufacturer offers systems to allow the planted roof to be specified by architects as easily as they would specify a flat roofing system.[9] Two types of roof are offered: the 'intensive', which is the equivalent of a normal garden with trees and plants and needs the same level of maintenance; and the 'extensive', which is light in weight and uses slow-growing plant species and therefore requires little or no maintenance.

The build-up of a commercial green roof

will depend on the roof area and its degree of slope.

8 Filter layer to prevent soil particles blocking the drainage.

9 Soil and planting.

A roof to take lawns and small shrubs will have a soil depth of 100 mm and, when saturated, will put a load on the structure of up to 1.15 kN/m^2. A roof that will take large bushes will have a soil depth of 350 mm and a loading of at least 4.0 kN/m^2. It is also possible to order pre-planted roofs, with small meadow flowers and grasses or pre-turfed roofs. These are said to need cutting only once a year, and have loadings of 0.8 and 0.65 kN/m^2 respectively. Such loadings can be compared with concrete roofing tiles which, with underfelt and battens, have a dead load of 0.685 kN/m^2.[10] Obviously roof tiles are not used on a flat roof, but the figure provides a comparison between the loadings caused by a planted roof and those caused by a more widely known roofing material.

Solarhaus, Issum

Such a planted roof is used on the Solarhaus at Issum in Germany.[11] It is laid to a slight slope, with the two pitches draining towards the middle. This avoids the problem of how to detail the edge of an earth-covered roof while allowing the water to drain off. With the drain in the centre, the edges of the roof can be finished with simple upstands to retain the soil. The roof of the Solarhaus has a timber structure carrying 120 mm of insulation topped with 150 mm of soil, to give a U value of 0.33 W/m^{2}K. This is a surprisingly poor level of insulation for a roof, but the house achieves good energy-saving performance by

The planted roof of the Solarhaus, Issum, resembles a small meadow. The house was designed by the owner, an energy consultant, with such experimental energy saving features as windows with a choice of blinds – thick or thin according to need – running between the inner and outer panes.
Architect: Haefs/Platen

virtue of its special window design, which gives an overall U value of 0.75 W/m²K, allowing the house to show an overall reduction of energy demand of 77 per cent compared to a conventionally constructed building of the same form.

The concept of 'touch-this-earth-lightly' embodies far more than respect for the site. A green roof is environmentally preferable to one of asphalt because it creates space for plants and insects, and these will provide food for birds, and even habitats for small mammals if the roof is large enough. It is a way of putting back a little of what the building has taken from the site. However, if the roof is to be more than a token gesture, it must be the roof of a building that 'touches-this-earth-lightly' in its demand for resources and energy. It is not just a question of respecting site. For the green architect the site is the whole planet.

Principle 6

Holism

All the green principles need to be embodied in a holistic approach to the built environment.

It is not easy to find buildings that embody all the principles of green architecture, for a green architecture is yet to be realized. Nevertheless, the following two buildings are described to show that it is possible to construct an architecture that embraces the majority of the principles.

Woodhouse Medical Centre, Sheffield

Completed in the spring of 1989, this building was then the largest superinsulated building in the UK.[1] Up to the time of its construction the doctors of Woodhouse, a suburb of the city of Sheffield, practised medicine from a converted house and a near-derelict chapel. The two practices came together with the local dentist to build a

centre that would improve conditions for patients as well as medical staff.

Under the National Health Service, general practitioners in Britain can build new premises provided that they meet certain enforceable criteria. From the architect's point of view, the most important of these criteria are concerned with building area, room requirements and overall cost. The number, type and size of rooms that a given medical practice is allowed to build are very strictly controlled, and the Regional Medical Officer must approve the proposed plans in terms of the inter-relationship of rooms. The overall area of building that is allowed is also fixed, and this determines the total sum allowed for the construction. The only flexibility in the cost is that additional allowance may be made for abnormal site conditions. The permitted cost is not high: it is comparable with the cost per square metre of building a reasonable quality house.

Within these constraints, the architect has complete freedom to design, provided that the clients are satisfied. The architects for the Medical Centre wanted to make a building with minimal environmental impact, and

Woodhouse Medical Centre, Sheffield. Angled buttresses mark divisions between the three sections and tie the building visually to the earth

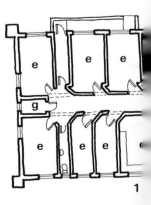

1

were interested to demonstrate that this could be done within a budget that was intended to build only a conventional building. The methods of reducing the building's impact were chosen as follows:

1   Use of maximum levels of insulation to reduce demand for fossil fuels.
2   Use of high efficiency heating systems to make the best use of the fossil fuel input to the building.
3   A thermally heavy structure to absorb casual and solar gains and provide good acoustic separation between rooms.
4   Use of UK manufactured materials wherever possible to reduce transport demands and provide employment.
5   No use of tropical hardwoods, to avoid destruction of the rainforests.
6   Choice of materials with low manufacturing energy demands.
7   Use of structural timber to lock up carbon taken from the atmosphere.
8   Choice of materials that would have a long life, with minimum maintenance.

These factors were set alongside the normal considerations that affect any architectural design activity and an effort was made to consider all decisions in terms of environmental questions.

The proposed site was an area of grassland sloping down from the south to a main road on the north. The constraints of the site led to an early decision to make the building relatively long and thin, in order to provide on the site the number of car parking spaces

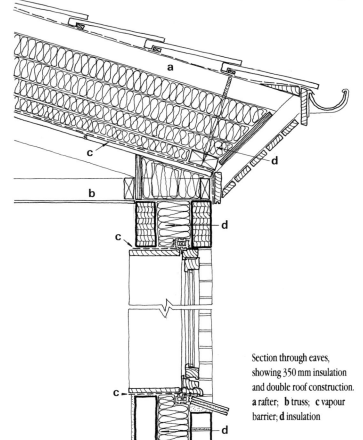

Section through eaves, showing 350 mm insulation and double roof construction. **a** rafter; **b** truss; **c** vapour barrier; **d** insulation

BELOW
Eaves and corner buttress

Plan of the Medical Centre:
a entry lobby; **b** reception; **c** office; **d** waiting room; **e** medical rooms; **f** staff room; **g** store

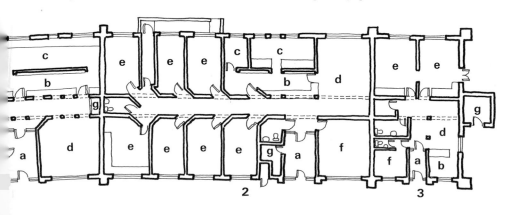

required by the Planning Authority. It was also planned that a separate clinic would be built on the site by the local Health Authority, and the proposed surgery building had to take account of this. A square building plan would offer a lower ratio of heated volume to heat-losing surface, but it would have wasted much of the space on the site. The site plan as designed uses the Medical Centre and the Clinic to create an open area, round which runs a footpath which provides access to the new buildings and continues an existing route across the site to the local shops.

The proposed envelope for the Medical Centre, a block about 12 metres wide and 60 metres long, with the long axis running up the north-south slope, had a number of advantages. It allowed a potentially economical layout with a central corridor and naturally lit rooms on both sides. The slope of the site meant that many of the windows would be above pedestrian eye-level so as to improve privacy, which can be in conflict with the need for light in a consulting room. The width of 12 metres allowed a simple (and therefore cheap) pitched roof to be used.

A building with a corridor down the mid-dle and rooms on each side may well be cheap, but it is not usually a particularly pleasant environment. The architects tried to break down the sense of being in a corridor by opening this area up to the underside of the roof and providing rooflights to give good natural daylight. Panes of glass let into the sides of the corridor near the roof allow daylight into the back of the rooms on either side, to supplement the light through the windows. The doors to all the consulting rooms were placed at an angle of 45 degrees to the corridor to break up the corridor further, and to ensure that the doors could be seen easily by patients walking along it.

The building was planned as three completely separate units, with no interconnection. This allowed the existing medical and dental practices to continue working in the ways that they had already established, and to keep the sense of personal attention to patients that they felt came from being each a small unit, while sharing the cost advantages that came from constructing one large building rather than three small ones.

Structurally the Woodhouse Medical Centre is simple; it has loadbearing masonry

Roof windows admit sunlight to the internal corridor of the Medical Centre. The wooden structure is not disguised, any more than are the thick brick walls that store heat gains from the patients and the sun

external walls and loadbearing walls along the central corridor, creating four parallel lines of support. Continuous beams of glue-laminated softwood (glulam) sit on top of the walls and carry timber half-trusses which are joined by rafters over the top of the corridor area. The timbers are all visible inside the building. Most rooms have flat ceilings, but in places the ceilings are cut away to allow light in via roof windows, revealing the trusses like bones beneath the skin. The glulam beams make efficient use of relatively small sections of timber which are laminated together for increased strength and uniformity, compared to solid timber of the same dimensions. The beams are all 100 mm by 215 mm, used in pairs with 25 mm black-stained plywood spacers between them. In one part of the building the span required is too great for this size of beam, and a steel flitch plate replaces the ply spacer to increase the allowed span of the beam. The pairs of beams and the spacers are held together with pieces of beechwood broom-handle used as connecting dowels, but where the flitch plate is used it is made obvious by the replacement of the dowels by bolts.

The exposed external lintels are also glulam, and are protected against rot by rods of solid boron-based wood preservative placed in holes in the ends of the lintels and plugged with small dowels. Boron is the least toxic of the common preservatives, and is released only if water enters the timber and dissolves the rods. If the timber does not reach a high enough water content to produce a risk of damage, the boron remains inactive.

The design of the Medical Centre is based on a simple approach to energy conservation. It uses traditional UK construction methods with only slight modifications to upgrade their performance, the reasoning being that typical contractors would not be faced, when tendering for the work, with practices that seemed very out-of-the-ordinary, and would not therefore increase their prices to compensate for the unfamiliarity of the work. The fact that the Medical Centre was constructed within the budget allowed for producing a building with no green features would seem to endorse this approach to design.

Heat loss through the ground floor was reduced by putting a 150 mm layer of expanded polystyrene (containing no CFCs) under the floor slab, giving a U value of 0.15 W/m²deg C. The slab was reinforced to span between the structural walls because of the slope of the site. (A large quantity of hardcore was needed to make up the levels, and it was deemed unwise to use this to support the slab in case of settlement.) The slab is power floated to provide a smooth surface to take floor finishes directly, without the need for a screed topping.

The external walls were made of facing brickwork with an inner skin of lightweight concrete blocks. This is the commonest form of construction in Britain for small buildings, and has the advantages of long life and low maintenance. The bricks chosen were made quite close to the site, so that transport costs, energy demand and pollution were reduced. The current Code of Practice for masonry walls allowed a maximum cavity width of 150 mm without the need to submit calculations to prove that the two leaves of the wall can still be considered to be acting in unison to support the building. This width was therefore chosen, and the entire space was filled with resin bonded glassfibre insulation batts. Stainless steel vertical twist type wall ties (available off-the-shelf in Sheffield for this cavity width) were placed at 450 mm centres vertically and horizontally. This gave a U value for the wall of about 0.2 W/m²deg C (compared with the value of 0.6 required by the Building Regulations applicable at the time). The facing bricks used were the most frost resistant (FL grade); because of all the insulation, it is likely that the external walls, not receiving warmth from inside the building, will be frozen for much of the winter, and lesser grades of bricks might suffer frost damage.

Windows were an off-the-peg 'high performance' type, incorporating draught seals and adjustable trickle vents in the heads to allow greater control of air movement in spring and autumn. They were designed to take 20 mm thick double-glazing units fixed with beads. In order to minimize the heat loss through the glazing without increasing the glazing-unit thickness, units were made that were 20 mm thick using two panes of 4 mm glass with a low-emissivity coating plus a 12 mm cavity filled with argon gas, to give a U value of 1.6 W/m²deg C.

At jambs and cills, the cavity was not closed to avoid the possibility of cold bridging through blockwork returns, which would offer less resistance to the passage of heat than the 150 mm insulation with which the wall was filled. At the heads of openings, the use of completely separate inner and outer lintels of glulam timber removed the danger of cold bridging that would arise with the use of conventional pressed steel lintels. The wooden lintels also allowed the clear' expression of the loadbearing elements, both internally and externally.

The windows used were made in the UK, and were not of as high a quality as standard Scandinavian windows which were becoming available in Britain. Herein lies the dilemma for the would-be ecological designer. There is no precise equation to show, for example, whether it is preferable to use locally made components (but of imported timber) to reduce transportation and provide employment, or to import more efficient and durable energy-saving components at possibly greater immediate environmental cost. The essence of green architecture is not that there is a single correct answer in any situation, but that designers should be aware of the factors to be evaluated when materials and components are specified.

The construction of the roof provided the greatest departure from conventional practice. In a previous low energy surgery building, the architects had used a polythene vapour barrier applied to the underside of the rafters and sealed at the joints with a non-setting mastic. This had been difficult to construct, as the builders had to work with the polythene above their heads and it had a tendancy to drop down on them. In addition, the fitting of the insulation between the rafters, with the depth of readily available timber limited to 200 mm, also limited to 200 mm the insulation that could easily be incorporated, and further layers had to be applied on top of the rafters to increase the U value.

The two problems led to a search for a new form of roof construction at the Medical Centre. The solution that was adopted, following close consultation with the structural engineer, was a two-layer roof. On top of the trusses was fixed a layer of water-resistant chipboard to form a smooth decking over which a vapour barrier was laid. (An imported Scandinavian material with woven reinforcement was used.) The joints were sealed with a purpose made double-sided tape to give an extremely strong bond. Once the vapour barrier was in place, the building was effectively waterproof. The next step was to nail horizontal timber bearers through the chipboard to the trusses. To these was fixed a completely separate roof structure made up of 50 mm by 100 mm rafters carrying conventional sarking felt, battens and concrete tiles. The rafters were fastened to the timber bearers with double-ended spacing screws which allowed them to be fixed at a set distance from the bearers, leaving a space of 350 mm to be filled with mineral fibre insulation. There was a gap of 100 mm above the insulation which was ventilated at eaves and ridge to remove any moisture that might enter the roof. The U value of the completed roof was 0.09 W/m²deg C. At the time the Medical Centre was completed, UK Building Regulations called for a value of 0.35 for a roof.

When the levels of insulation in the fabric of a building are high, an elemental analysis of heat losses shows that the greatest single source of heat loss is due to casual ventilation (draughts). The first technique of draught-reduction is the use of an effective air-vapour barrier, particularly on areas of the building that are of framed construction such as a roof. (Plastered masonry walls are sufficiently airtight not to constitute a problem.) The vapour barrier at the Medical Centre is sealed to the walls at all perimeters to avoid any air leakage at these points, and it was largely the desire to create a satisfactory seal at all remaining points that prompted the design of the roof construction. Vapour barriers were also fixed round all window linings to ensure that air could not enter the building through the cavity of the wall, even though this was filled with insulation.

The second technique is to seal components to one another. In the case of a masonry building this is relatively simple, because the use of a wet construction tends to create a fairly well sealed skin. However where elements like windows and doors are inserted they must be sealed to the rest of the building with appropriate sealants.

The third method is to ensure that any elements that open are fitted with effective draught seals, so that they admit air only when the users of the building want air: the gap round a typical closed external door is equivalent to having a brick missing from the wall. At the Medical Centre the elements that came ready made were fitted with seals at the factory; other components such as the doors were fitted with seals in long-lived materials such as neoprene – a case where high-tech materials have a role to play in ecological architecture. Even the letterboxes were fitted with draught seals. All external doors were provided with draught lobbies so that entry or exit did not remove excessive quantities of warm air. Considerable care was taken that the draught lobbies should be large enough to make it impossible to open both doors at once and thereby defeat the lobby's purpose.

Finally, it is necessary to provide a method of ventilation without increasing heat loss, and at the Medical Centre heat exchangers are linked to mechanical ventilation units, one for each of the three blocks of the building. The stream of outgoing stale but heated air passes through the heat exchanger where it gives up its heat to the incoming fresh but cold air, providing satisfactory ventilation and reducing heat loss due to ventilation by about 70 per cent. (In the heat loss calculations a value of about 0.2 air changes per hour can be used, which is the thermal effect corresponding to a much higher level of ventilation in terms of fresh air input.) Each room in the Centre has an air extract, and some also have a fresh air supply. Where there is no supply, fresh air is drawn in under the door of the room from the rest of the building as the stale air is extracted.

The effect of the energy saving techniques outlined above is to reduce the heat loss from the building to a total of 512 W/K (watts per degree of temperature difference), which gives a value for the heated volume of 0.28 $W/m^3/K$. If the Medical Centre had been constructed in accordance with then-current Building Regulations the total loss would have been 2,089 W/K; that is, about four times greater. Under the revised UK Building Regulations brought in on 1 April 1990, which are supposed to improve thermal performance, the heat loss would still be 1,970 W/K. The reduction in heating demand achieved by the Medical Centre is 76 per cent compared to the old Regulations, and 74 per cent compared to the new. Had the Medical Centre been built to meet the old Building Regulations, the heat loss from the glazing alone would be greater than the heat loss from the whole Centre as built.

Heating to the building is provided by three separate central heating systems, one in each block. Each system uses low water content radiators for fast response to control, with thermostatic valves on each radiator to turn it off when the space reaches the desired temperature. The radiators are fed by a wall-hung gas fired condensing boiler which extracts the latent heat from the water vapour in the flue gases to achieve very high combustion efficiency. The boiler works most effectively when the temperature of the returning water in the circuit is low, so the radiators are about 20 per cent oversized to help achieve this. The water-temperature reduction is also helped by the fact that the whole system is physically much larger than the 8.5 kW boiler would normally operate, with long pipe runs and seventeen radiators. The boiler used is of a rating that would normally be put into a small house. The larger blocks of the building have a heat loss of 5.6 kW at a temperature difference of 25 degrees. The average efficiency of the boiler in use is quoted as 85 per cent under standard conditions, rising to over 90 per cent with lower flow-and-return temperatures; this compares with about 70 per cent for standard boilers. The use of condensing boilers alone reduces the delivered energy consumption for space heating by 15 per cent.

Hot water is not supplied by the boilers, because a long thin building with washbasins in nearly every room cannot easily be supplied with hot water from a central source. In the consulting rooms, doctors and nurses need to be able to rinse their hands but not to run a sink full of water. If the water came from a central source a lot of cold water would have to be run off before it reached the tap hot, so a decision was made to use electric under-sink water heaters to supply temperature-controlled hot water at the point of use. It is not efficient in primary energy terms to use electricity for heating, but in this case a value judgement had to be made about relative energy use.

Lighting energy use has also been considered in the design of the building. It was thought inappropriate to use fluorescent strip lights as these would create too much of an institutional atmosphere, but tungsten lights produce too much heat. The decision was made to use compact fluorescent lamps in a variety of fittings. The result is a saving in lighting energy demand of 80 per cent.

Finally, it is appropriate to describe the architectural expression of the Medical Centre. In order to achieve the required ecological aspects of the design within a fixed budget it was essential that the design remained simple. The choice of form – a rectangular shed, and materials – brick, concrete tiles and timber windows, was determined by the need for economy in initial cost as well as, in the case of materials, economy in energy of manufacture and maintenance. The brick shed with a pitched roof that resulted is modified by the use of angled brick buttresses at the corners and at the junctions between the three blocks. These are used to tie the building visually to the earth by breaking the abrupt transition from horizontal ground to vertical wall. Against the slope of the buttresses and the 1:12 fall of the site, the building's horizontality is emphasized by the use of brick bands at floor, cill and head level.

The Arts and Crafts dictum that one should do nothing to a material except that which honours it best has been the driving force behind the architectural expression. Everything is what it seems to be, and materials have been used deliberately to express aspects of construction that are usually hid-

den. Wooden lintels support the brick walls over openings; the pegs that join the inner and outer lintels project visibly from the faces on both sides (but, being timber they cause no cold bridge); creasing tiles form drips and cills where needed to keep rain from the timber, and small dowels reveal the location of boron preservative rods. Internally the timber beams that can be seen, while decorative, are the beams that support the building. Where the ceilings are cut away to reveal the skeletal trusses behind, they are standard trusses with the usual imperfections; they have not been specially treated for display. The sloping eaves provides a visual link with the sloping buttresses, but also shows the thickness of the superinsulated roof construction, and reveals where air can enter to ventilate the roof voids above the insulation. Internally, white painted plaster and stained timber provide the simplest possible background for the pictures and hangings provided by the users, and reflect the sunlight that streams through the roof windows to reduce the need for electric light.

The building, because of the nature of the industry which operates at this scale of construction, is a craft product, but it is made of standard mass-produced components, and an attempt is made to express this, also. It is a demonstration that it is possible to produce a green building within existing parameters and technologies.

NMB Bank headquarters

The second building chosen as embodying most of the green principles is a project on a vastly different scale. In 1978 the NMB Bank decided to build a new headquarters in a suburb in the south east of Amsterdam.[2] In Britain or the United States most organizations rent their office space. Buildings are put up as investments by speculative developers who benefit both from the rents that they can charge and from the increasing market value of their buildings, against which can borrow to finance further developments. The NMB Bank followed the very different Dutch and German pattern of office development.

BUILDING WITH LOCAL MATERIALS

RIGHT, ABOVE
47 Eaves of the Woodhouse Medical Centre, Sheffield. Their depth is one of the few visual clues to the building's superinsulated construction. Decoration is derived purely from the materials used – local bricks and clay tiles – and the way they are put together

RIGHT, BELOW
48 Top of a circulation tower, NMB Bank headquarters building, Amsterdam. The use of traditional Dutch brick lends a human scale to an office development the size of a small town. Pentagonal solar collectors on the roof preheat ventilation air

OVERLEAF
49 The NMB Bank headquarters took its shape from a variety of green principles, including consultative planning. The result is a highly distinctive-looking building that is the pride of all involved with it

INSET, LEFT TO RIGHT
50–52 Informal meetings are encouraged by a design of generous public spaces. Durable natural materials such as the marble for the floors are not confined to reception lobbies, but extend to all the public areas. Offices have good daylighting and flexible spaces to encourage working in small groups

53 The glazed roof of an NMB Bank circulation tower allows sunlight to pour down into the linking street below

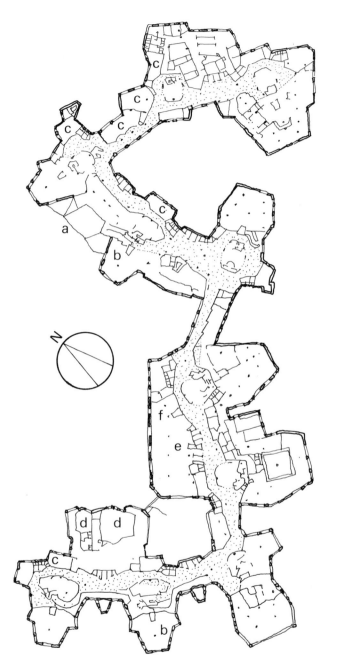

Layout of NMB Bank, showing the wide internal street running through the centre of the building. Major spaces include: a entry; b restaurant; c meeting room; d public relations centre; e post room; f print room

By this custom, a firm wanting a new office borrows money from a bank, appoints an architect or holds an architectural competition, and builds its own specially designed office building to suit its own needs.

NMB is one of the three largest banks in the Netherlands, and needed a large building to accommodate 2,000 staff. The choice of site was the result of a vote among the staff, who were able to opt for the location that would provide the easiest journey to work for the majority. The same degree of participation was carried through to many other aspects of the design process. Workers' Councils have the right under Dutch law to be involved when an employer plans to make changes to the working environment. The people who were to work in the new bank were not simply told to transfer to the new building on a certain date, as would have been likely in Britain or the USA. They were involved in design and technical considerations such as the need for a view to the outside, and the desire to have opening windows rather than air conditioning. They also discussed the materials of the building; the result is careful use of 'natural' materials wherever possible, and avoidance of materials that are polluting in manufacture, such as foamed plastics made with CFCs, or that may have hazards in use, such as chipboard that emits formaldehyde gas.

The involvement of the users of the building in its design was one aspect of an alternative approach to the design process, but of equal importance in the creation of the finished work was the unusual organization of the design team. The conventional model for the design of a large office block is that the architect is in control of the whole design, and calls in consultants to provide the technical detail for areas that are outside the architect's competence. For example, a services engineer might design the electrical system, a structural engineer would ensure that the building will stand up, and so on. The architect for the NMB Bank, Ton Alberts of Amsterdam, took a much less central role in the design team than is usual. The team who produced the design for the building included a representative appointed by the Bank to

oversee the whole process of building procurement from the client's point of view; the
architect; the structural engineer; a building
physicist; interior design consultants; acoustic advisers and landscape designers. While
this is not an unusual team to be assembled
for the design of a large, complex building,
there was none of the conventional hierarchy
that might be found in such a team. Each
member of the group was able to comment
on the input of any other member, and the
whole team was responsible for the final
design. The consultative structure avoided
the usual situation where different consultants may be in conflict with one another and
with the architect. It mirrors the involvement
of the users, as part of the democratization
of the process of design. Each member of the
team provided his or her particular expertise,
and was still responsible for the detailed
design of particular aspects of the building,
but the design was the result of the creative
interaction of all the design team members.

The obvious criticism of this approach,
from those used only to the normal method
of proceeding, is that it would result in
'design by committee', giving a bland and
uninteresting building as the final result.
Because of the commitment of the Bank to
produce a high quality and ecologically
sound building, combined with the enthusiasm of the design team for these concepts
and for the novel design process, the result is
a building that is unlike any other. Rather
than a bland, inoffensive form, the NMB Bank
has acquired a headquarters which is
instantly recongnizable and uniquely suited
to its needs. The involvement of the staff
throughout the design process also reduces
the sense of alienation that can result when
people are forced to move into a building
that is not of their choosing. The whole
design process has stimulated rather than
stifled creativity.

The NMB Bank is of necessity a large building. It has about 50,000 m^2 of floor space plus
a further 28,000 m^2 of basement car parking.
It is nearly a kilometre in length. Built as a
traditional office block set down in a modest
suburb, such a volume of space would have
an enormously destructive impact. Instead of

The NMB in its
neighbourhood. Note the
contrast with office blocks of
conventional design

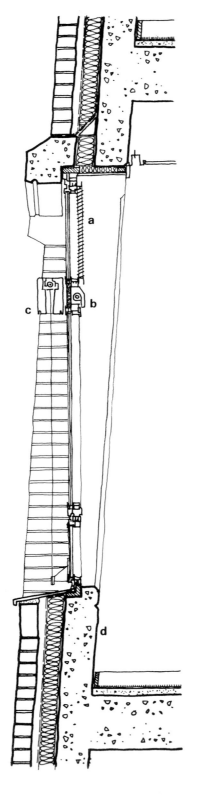

NBM Bank, section through
external wall and window:
a louvred light deflector;
b internal blind, manually
operated; **c** computer
operated external blind;
d concrete structure

building a large block (which might have
been the cheapest solution in simplistic
economic terms) the designers have broken
the office accommodation into a series of ten
individual but linked units, each centred on a
small glass roofed space containing stairs and
a lift. The lifts and stairs are linked by a curving internal street that runs down the centre
of the building at ground level. Off this street
are restaurants, meeting rooms, a cinema and
other shared facilities, with the office spaces
above.

No two blocks of office accommodation
are the same. They vary in height, plan shape
and orientation, although each working
space is designed to allow groups of roughly
twenty people to work together. These
groups are the basis of the Bank's working
organization. There is no sign of the rigid rectangular layout of a typical British or US office
with its obsession with movable partitioning
to allow any occupier to alter it to fit. The
NMB building is designed specifically for one
user, and while the user might have problems if it were to change radically the way it
wished to organize its activities, this is unlikely to happen. Moreover, the NMB building provides space that could be used by a
variety of organizations in a variety of ways.
Flexibility is produced, not by making all the
walls movable as in the conventional speculative office block, but by making spaces of a
size for groups of people to work together.

The great advantage that the NMB building
has in organizational terms over the conventional rectangular block is that the designers
have deliberately created spaces with which
individuals can identify. This approach to
office organization was pioneered by the
Dutch architect Herman Hertzberger in his
Centraal Beheer building. Within a building
for a large organization, Hertzberger managed to create a sense of individual spaces for
individual users without partitioning the
space into little cells. People had space that
they could personalize, but they were also
recongnizably part of a larger space and a
larger organization.

The people who work there in the NMB
building are occupants of a building that
holds 2,000 workers, but the division of this

Each of the NMB Bank
circulation towers has a
different form, but all have
prominent stairways to
encourage walking up rather
than using the elevator

large block into ten separate units has created something akin to a small town. Each of these units is centred on the circulation tower through which light enters, and each tower holds the stairs and lifts. The height of the blocks is low enough that using the stair is the preferred means of movement, and the design of the stairs encourages this, with emphasis placed on them rather than on the lifts. The blocks of offices are further differentiated from one another by their differing orientations and their different views over the landscaped gardens. The gardens help to connect the artificially created town of the Bank with the real suburb where it is situated, and provide benefit both to office workers looking out and local residents looking in.

The ten buildings of this artificial town are joined together on all floor levels, but the street at ground level is the major linking element. As it curves between the blocks it provides a series of views of the different gardens, alternating with light coming from the rooflit access towers of the office blocks. The most striking aspects of this street are its scale and richness of detailing. In a speculative office building the circulation space is seen as 'unprofitable' because it is not bringing in rent. The result is that it is reduced to a minimum. There may be a lobby on the ground floor with a marble floor to create an impression of luxury at the entrance, but that is usually the limit. At the NMB building the circulation space is designed to be an enjoyable experience. It is architecturally stimulating, and filled with sculpture, plants and water. There is no sense of penny-pinching.

The headquarters of the NMB Bank is undeniably striking as a work of architecture. In avoiding the form and appearance of a conventional office block, the design team has gone to the opposite extreme and produced a building in which no two lines are parallel or vertical. The result is a building that is unique and immediately recognizable. It acts as publicity for the Bank merely by virtue of its existence. By breaking the space down into units that are almost domestic in scale, the designers have avoided the need for complex structural systems, and have been able to use a simple reinforced con-

crete frame, externally finished in brick. This enhances the domestic feel of the building, and continues the Dutch tradition of exquisite brickwork detailing used to create expressionist forms, typified by the work of the Amsterdam School in the early part of the twentieth century. It is unusual to see this approach to architecture used to create an office building. Visually, the sloping walls help to tie the building to the ground by making its emergence less abrupt. They also serve to reduce the impact on the surroundings by allowing the Bank to taper away from its neighbours rather than loom over them.

The breaking down of the plan into smaller, more intimate areas has been followed through in the design of every element. There are no standard solutions endlessly repeated, as would be found in most offices. Each block is subtly different in detailing and colour scheme, but all make use of the same architectural language. The result is variety within a formal framework.

The NMB Bank would be remarkable for its attempts to respond to users, its democratic design team and its appearance alone, but it is also, according to the Dutch building research organization TNO, the most energy efficient office building in the world. The energy efficiency starts with the construction, which uses materials such as brick and reinforced concrete which are in themselves low in manufacturing energy content. The design team were enabled to make use of such materials because their planning had created a building form which did not need wide spans or advanced cladding systems; this is another example of the benefit when all the consultants are acting together.

The floors are in reinforced concrete, as are the 180 mm-thick inner leaves of the external walls. This high mass structure is wrapped round with 100 mm of mineral fibre insulation with a cavity of 30 mm on the external face and an outer skin of brickwork. The mass of the building helps to give good acoustic performance, but its principal task is to even out temperature fluctuations by absorbing heat gains from people, computers, lights and sunlight, and giving warmth out later when the spaces start to cool.

The double-glazed windows are metal framed, with a coloured finish to reduce maintenance needs. The possibilities of cold bridging are reduced by the inclusion of thermal breaks in the frames. Cold bridging has also been avoided in the window reveals by careful separation of the inner and outer leaves of the external wall construction. Thermal breaks of rigid insulation are used between inner and outer lintels, with the addition of separate insulated linings to the window openings.

The windows were one of the design elements affected by the comments of the people who were to work in the building. They wanted good natural lighting and natural ventilation, and also to exclude external noise. The design team had to meet these requirements while avoiding excessive heat loss or overheating through the large window areas typically required for high levels of daylight. The result was a window design that allowed overall glazing area to be limited to 20 per cent of the external wall area, while giving highly satisfactory lighting levels of 500 Lux. The natural lighting was enhanced by the provision of a fixed pane of glass at the top of the window, backed by reflecting louvres. These louvres, looking like silvered venetian blinds, reflect daylight on to the ceiling of the room which further reflects it into the back of the space. These windows, together with the designers' care to ensure that no workplace is more than 7 metres from a window, contribute to the building's low energy needs during daylight hours. The layout of the ten office towers ensures that all receive sunlight at some period of the day. This helps to reduce heating demands during the winter months, but it can be undesirable from an energy point of view in summer. The building is equipped with computer-controlled sunblinds on the outer face of the glazing to eliminate unwanted solar gain, and internal blinds can be operated by the occupants if they find the sunlight too strong (see p. 164).

The windows are a good example of the integrated design approach. The users wanted the pleasure of views and sunlight in their workplaces, as well as comfortable working conditions; the designers want to achieve good energy performance. The care given to the design of the glazing allowed these often mutually exclusive demands to work together to give good light and views without resorting to a highly glazed and energy-losing façade.

Glazing is also important in the roof. The access towers to the offices have glazed tops to allow light to filter down to the internal street, but large areas of roof glazing are also used as part of the energy system of the building. Pentagonal glazed areas collect solar energy which is used to pre-heat the ventilation air to the building, so that at an external air temperature of 7 degrees C, the internal temperature can be 21 degrees C without the use of any additonal energy from the central boiler plant, which has a rated output of 1,000 kW.

The heat is derived not only from solar energy, but also from a heat store in the basement consisting of 100 cubic metres of water in four large insulated tanks. The tanks are heated partly by waste heat from the building's own electrical generators, fuelled by gas or oil. By making its own electricity and collecting the waste heat the Bank can make use of energy normally wasted in the generation of electricity. The heat stores also collect waste heat from sources such as the lift machinery and the computer equipment. By 'dumping' waste heat into the insulated tanks, the plant operators can save it for use when it is needed inside the building, rather than allowing it to be uselessly dissipated.

Energy is also saved by the fact that the building has no air conditioning plant. The workers in the building wanted to have control over their environment, and they called for opening windows and simple controls that would allow them to adjust the system in local areas to their own liking. A speculatively built office would be likely to have air conditioning installed as a norm, and have higher running costs in consequence. If current thinking on 'sick building syndrome' is correct, it would not necessarily lead to better working conditions, and air conditioning installations are also implicated in many outbreaks of Legionnaires' disease. By opting for a building without air conditioning, the workers at NMB have avoided possible problems and given themselves more control over their environment. The environmental control system mirrors the decentralized plan form and the decentralized planning process which created the building.

The success of the energy design can be shown by comparing the new NMB headquarters with the Bank's former building. The new building has a primary energy demand for the whole year of 111 kWh/m². The earlier building, completed in the 1970s, had a demand of 1,320 kWh/m². The saving in energy costs was about £1.3 million per year, but the additional cost attributable to the energy saving measures was less than a quarter of that sum.

It is easy to criticize the NMB Bank headquarters as yet another vast office development. In a future 'green' world, will there still be a role for huge organizations like the NMB Bank? Can a building be considered even remotely green if it has a large basement car park?

The real importance of the building is not that it solves every problem, but that it demonstrates there is another way. It shows that the users can have a meaningful involvement in the procurement of a new workplace, and that a big organization will not be destroyed by the process of consultation. It demonstrates that the conventional model of conflicting interests and rule by the architect is not the only approach to designing a large building. The pride of the Bank in the finished product suggests that an ecologically sound building can be prestigious. The extraordinary appearance of the building, inside and out, shows that environmental awareness and energy efficiency are no brake on architectural creativity; rather, they have served here as a stimulus to the design team.

PROPOSAL

Ground rules for the green city

A green architecture involves more than the individual building on its
plot; it must encompass a sustainable form of urban environment.
The city is far more than a collection of buildings; rather it can
be seen as a series of interacting systems – systems for living, working
and playing – crystallized into built forms.
It is by looking at systems that we can find the face of the city of
tomorrow.

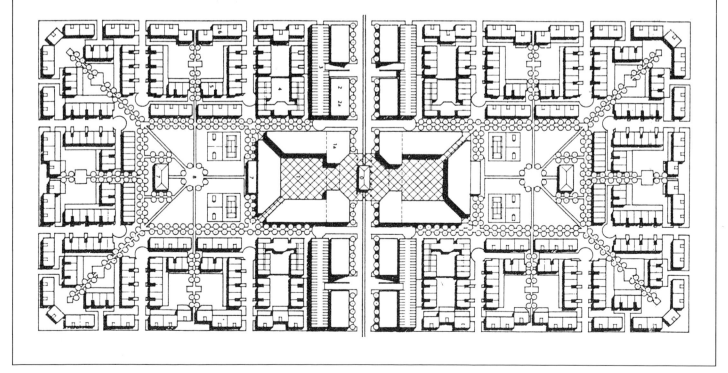

The overcrowding and squalor of the Victorian city, depicted by Gustave Doré in *Over London by Rail*

THERE have always been those ready to argue that it is possible for a single designer to create a plan for all or a substantial part of a city. At times such plans have been based on an intellectual proposal such as Le Corbusier's rationalization of transport:

> The tracks for fast motor traffic pass under the aerodrome. The unobstructed and open ground-floor levels of the skyscrapers can be seen, as can the piles or stilts on which they are built. Covered car-parking can be perceived on either side.[1]

Where the people are going, and why, is not considered. The need to cater for transport dominates the plan as if the transport had its own goal and motivation. At other times city designers have produced plans predicated on the need to create open space within the city to prevent crime, as in Victorian times attempts were made to open up crowded districts by demolishing selected houses to improve view and supervision. Later the poor were decanted into cottage estates on the edges of the city where gardens and open spaces alleviated the congestion, but also reduced the density of population that is the justification of the city. Perhaps most commonly, the plan of the single designer has evolved around a visual premise. Such ideas for improvement perhaps fail to recognize that what a person sees is conditioned by whom a person is, even by such a seemingly insignificant factor as whether he or she belongs to the neighbourhood or street or is foreign to it. Places which may seem unremittingly ugly to the visitor

are accepted by the residents because they are overlaid with layers of the residents' own history. When areas of cities are cleared for wholesale redevelopment they take part of the lives of the inhabitants with them.

To propose a simple 'green' approach to the creation of cities would therefore be as naïve as some of the proposals of the past. A theoretical examination of the green city must take account of the overwhelming complexity of city structure before any alternatives can be put forward.

In essence the city represents the most extreme example of not working with nature

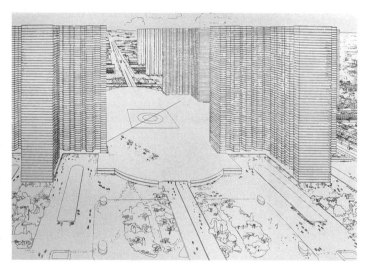

RIGHT, ABOVE
Earlier this century, Le Corbusier's 'Central Station', was a vision of the city totally dominated by the need for transportation, represented here by car, train and plane

RIGHT
The French architect Tony Garnier's industrial city plan was based on rigorous zoning. By siting housing area away from the industrial area and city centre, it removed much of the richness of traditional city life along with some of its squalor. Personal transport is still a necessity

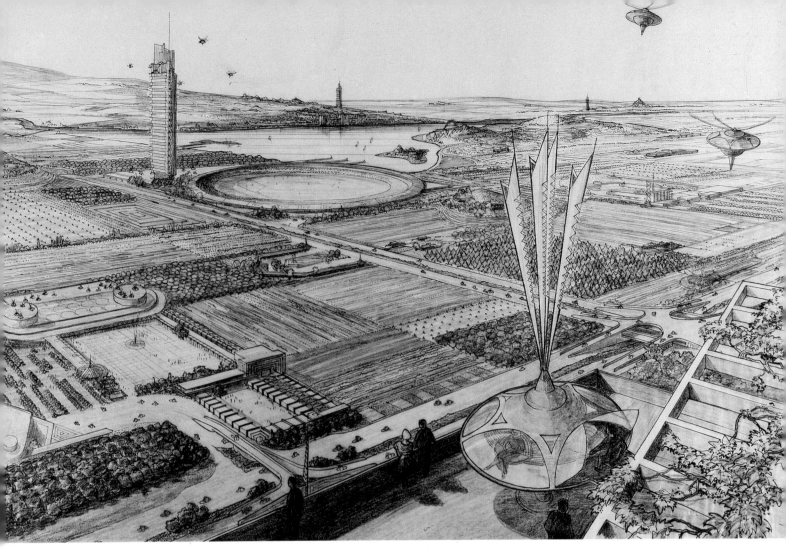

that people have yet produced on the planet. Even though agriculture throughout the world alters the natural environment, with the inevitable consequences to the indigenous flora and fauna, it has to take account of soil, climate, predators and availability of people for production and consumption if it is to be sustainable. In other words, it has to take account of some natural systems. The city, however, has not taken account of a sustainable future since the time of the city under threat of siege, when sufficient land for growing food and a water supply had to be included within its defensible boundaries. The modern city relies upon a worldwide hinterland for the supply of materials to sustain it, and its wastes issue back into the environment, in some instances to pollute on an equally wide scale.

To talk of a green city, therefore, might seem an untenable concept. Although Frank Lloyd Wright's Broadacre City apparently addressed the idea of each citizen being allocated a sufficient tract of land (land in a quantity that could support many families of the squatter settlements around many of the world's modern cities),[2] the proposal was essentially visually based. The inhabitants of Broadacre City needed personal transport to provide the contacts between many people that form the essence of any city:

> Every Broadacre citizen has his own car. Multiple lane highways make travel safe and enjoyable.[3]

Such a vision with its emphasis on decentralization of facilities and government almost reaches the point of negating the city. A similar proposal in another context may be seen as a vision of rural rather than city life. The Ministry of Labour in Germany under National Socialism in 1937 put forward a proposal for subsistence homesteading.[4] The workers were to live on the rural side of any factory, with subsistence farming provided for them in times of industrial unemployment on homesteads of a quarter of an acre. A

Frank Lloyd Wright's 'Broadacre' city plan gave an acre of land to every household, but the inhabitants still depended for communications on a motorway grid and a helicopter for every family

A National Socialist family on
its smallholding celebrates
the return of Father after a
hard day's work at the factory.
Now he must milk the cow
and continue with the
building of the house in the
background

RIGHT
Traditional architecture of
narrow streets, moderating
climate

similar scheme was initiated with the chari-
table settlement of Bournville in England, set
up for the employees of Cadbury in 1895,
where gardens of 600 square yards, sufficient
for a single man to cultivate, were provided to
supplement the industrial workers' incomes
and provide healthy recreation.

Such proposals are for a suburban rather
than an urban environment, and without the
high levels of personal transport envisaged
by Wright, provide an isolated rather than a
collective existence. A city must be a collection of many people in one place with sufficient buildings to shelter their activities if it
is to remain a city.

Nevertheless, the city can be made green
through the way in which it interacts with the
rest of the planet. The fundamental question
is one of examining each system that operates
within the urban context to see at which level
it functions in a way that parallels that of
nature. For example, a combined heat and
power system can operate at the scale of a single building or at the scale of a neighbourhood within a city. At the scale of a single
building or building complex it may be much
harder to match the demand for both heat
and power within a single unit, so that excess
power needs to be stored in some way (perhaps by feeding into a much larger electricity
supply system). At a scale somewhere between the neighbourhood and the whole city

it may be much easier to match supply and demand for power. This suggests that there may exist a scale for the built environment that will enable it to be arranged in sympathy with the energy supply.

Energy conservation, on the other hand, may be applied to any building within the city, whether to warm or cool. Many traditional areas of towns and cities have been given form through this simple response to climatic conditions, like the courtyard architecture of Marrakesh in Morocco, where buildings are clustered to provide shade for the streets and interiors of the buildings. The orientating of buildings to make use of solar energy on a city-wide scale can be seen in the plan for an industrial city by the French architect Tony Garnier, developed between 1901 and 1917. Here housing is placed along the contours of the south-west facing slope to take advantage of a solar aspect. The constraint on the layout of the houses and the

space around them has produced a geometric response to natural topography. The use of solar energy in cities is certainly feasible, but it may not be wise to dictate city form entirely by its exploitation.

In the Cité Industrielle, the fact that the mass of housing is zoned away from the city centre and industrial district only highlights the major constraint on recent city development: that of the need to provide a means of moving people around the city. The supply of power and energy may have some influence on the arrangement of the city; the supply of food may limit the size of green cities if the city hinterland is to provide food for the city population, but the economic basis of the city must depend upon an arrangement for transportation of goods and people, both within and beyond its boundaries.

The history of city development can be seen as no more than a reflection of the history of transportation, from the growth of coastal cities around ports to the development of inland cities that grew up along the trade routes. Within the city, however, it was the movement of the inhabitants on foot that dictated the arrangement of the buildings. This, when combined with the need to house as many people as possible within the walls for defensive purposes, produced a plan of narrow lanes separating buildings, with only the roads leading to the main gateways wide enough to allow horse, camel or ox drawn traffic to carry on the business of export and import. Around the harbour too the ways would be wide enough for horse-drawn traffic, the unloading of boats and the storage of goods, but just behind this area, buildings were separated by narrow pathways and steps for foot traffic only – the very feature that makes such settlements with their human scale for the built environment so attractive to people of a very different age.

As new forms of transport were developed, so cities responded and the pattern of built form altered. When central areas were cleared of slums and lodging houses to provide passage for the new railways with their termini, city development and enlargement followed the course of the rail or tram lines. Only with the comparative freedom of the

LEFT
Gardens at Bournville, England. Most city planting has only amenity value, but urban plots, however tiny, have the potential to produce a wide variety of foodstuffs

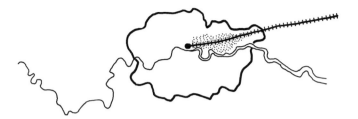

Housing development in London in the nineteenth-century following the line of the Great Eastern Railway. Cheap fares were offered to the displaced workers to encourage them to commute

motor bus did areas of the city between the lines become as attractive to live in.

Nevertheless, city development was still related to travel on foot, since the normal practice was to walk to a public transport stop. Once the private car became available to many more people, the scale of city development changed. Roads now needed to be wider, and a whole series of built environments to house the car, including garages, car parks and street parking, had to be slotted into existing cities. The demand for space for the car only reduced the room in which it could manoeuvre. The consequence is that cities designed to a human scale, in both the first and developing worlds, are now choked with traffic. It became necessary to create an order around the car, with the human order becoming subservient.

The grid city of Los Angeles is typical of such an organization. No travel is possible without the automobile, for the city sprawls across the land without regard to the time and distance associated with walking. This same model has been applied to the new city of Milton Keynes in England. A grid of roads has been imposed on the countryside, with local housing areas located in some grid squares and the major shopping area and city centre in others. In the area remaining between the roads, one million trees have been planted. In terms of energy balance, the quantity of carbon dioxide released by a typical car travelling ten thousand miles per year on journeys to work and shop will need some two hundred trees to absorb it. A million trees will therefore cope with the carbon dioxide emission from five thousand cars. However visually green it may appear, the city of a million trees organized around car travel can only be considered a 'green' city if its population does not exceed about twenty

Housing area with planting in the French architect Tony Garnier's industrial city plan

thousand (estimating one car to every four inhabitants).

The type of planting within the city can affect the overall energy balance. Planting at present has only an amenity value, and, although local levels of carbon dioxide are reduced around areas of urban planting, further reduction in global carbon dioxide levels could be achieved through substitution of plants grown for food, both to reduce transport energy use and give food grown without the aid of chemicals that themselves have a high energy content. There is the potential for the green city to become agriculturally productive. For vegetable growing, the gardener can raise more produce for the same area of land than the farmer,[5] and at a lower energy cost. However, closer spatial re-

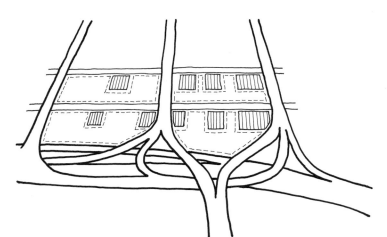

lationships will need to be formed between home, recreation and workplace, and the city to be fragmented into a series of neighbourhoods to allow the individual to move from one to the other on foot, or any energy savings will be lost.

A group of architects in the United States has proposed a scheme for the transformation of that most American of phenomena, the suburb.[6] One driving force behind the proposals is that the suburbs as they exist at present are designed for families with children, in spite of data from the United States Census Bureau that only 27 per cent of new households formed in the 1980s would be made up of married couples. The new households, whether single elderly people or single parents, often find that the conventional three-bedroomed family house is not suitable for their needs, but the developers are not building anything else. The suburbs, lacking public spaces, are also seen as a place where people are separated from any involvement in public life, and where activity revolves round the automobile. The relocation of employment to suburban locations to avoid the traffic jams of city centres has resulted in traffic congestion as bad as that in conventional urban areas, with the accompanying problems of high fuel consumption and pollution that people hoped to escape by moving to the suburbs in the first place. Low density suburbs are spreading across the country, using up farmland and creating ever increasing automobile dependence.

The solution to suburban alienation, according to architects Doug Kelbaugh and Peter Calthorpe, is the creation of 'pedestrian pockets', small communities located on a light rail line (a form of tram) that links them with each other and with existing urban centres. The pockets are designed to incorporate a mix of housing, shopping, community facilities and employment, with all buildings arranged to lie within a five minute walk of the station. The area of a typical pocket would be no more than 100 acres, containing housing for 5,000 people and jobs for 3,000. The density of fifty people per acre can be compared with the city of Milton

LEFT

Los Angeles: freeway elevated above the road grid and parking lots. In some parts of the city, roads and parking occupy more space than buildings (shaded areas)

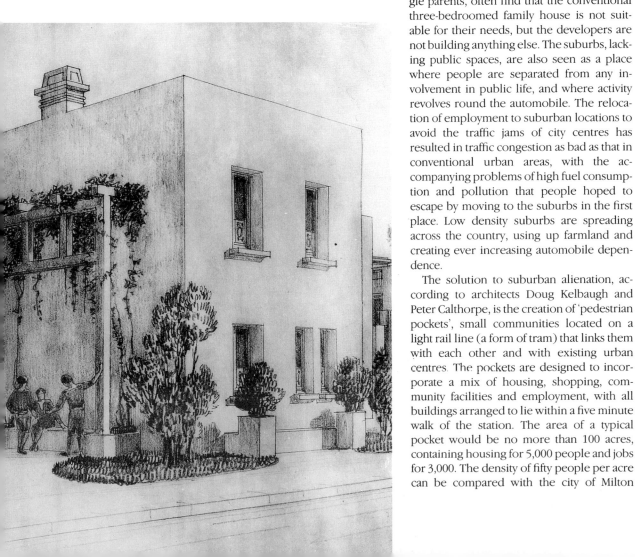

A fantasy solution to problems of urban pollution: Buckminster Fuller's proposal for a giant geodesic dome to shelter midtown Manhattan. A realistic programme would be the upgrading of all city buildings and systems, each according to need. But to take an area such as this, somewhat larger than a neighbourhood, may well make it easier to match power supply to demand

Low rise buildings and a light rail line at the centre of a 'pedestrian pocket'

Keynes in England which has a density of only eleven people per acre.[7] The density of the pockets is designed to ensure that there are enough people to make the light rail system viable, and to allow some of the vitality and human interaction provided by a traditional small town. The housing would be in the form of two- or three-storey terraces and apartments, while the offices, with shops under, would be no taller than four storeys.

Compared to a conventional new town, the pedestrian pocket is not meant to be self contained, it is more a way of containing development, and the links provided between pockets and existing settlements allow both communities to share the facilities of the other, with mutual benefit. Whereas in the conventional suburb people have no option but to drive to work, to school and to shops, in the pedestrian pocket people can walk, drive or take the light rail train.

The Department of Architecture at the University of Washington hosted a one week design 'workshop' in 1988, during which four teams of architects and students designed layouts for a pedestrian pocket near the town of Auburn. The idea has moved beyond the drawing board with the scheme by California developer Phil Angelidos together with Peter Calthorpe to construct a new development on 800 acres in Sacramento based on the pedestrian pocket concept.[8] Houses are at higher density than a normal suburb, and feature front porches and back alleys, with tree-lined narrow streets, in an attempt to recreate something of the atmosphere of small-town America. The first development in Laguna Creek will be joined by others in the same area. One reason for the interest in these ideas in California is that the air quality has become so poor because of automobile exhaust emissions that planners are looking for ways of reducing the number of journeys that people make.[9] The unknown factors are twofold; will people be prepared to live at higher densities, or do they really prefer the spacious suburbs that designers find so unsatisfactory; and secondly, will the citizens of California be persuaded to end their love affair with the automobile, and take to their feet instead? The fact that developers are putting money into these schemes suggests that they are confident that pedestrian pocket ideas will be a success.

The need to reduce levels of carbon dioxide and other pollutants entering the atmosphere demands a reconsideration of the spatial relations between the mass of population housed in the city, the resources required by these people, and the transportation necessary to move these people and resources about. No solution is offered here, except to suggest that cities can no longer continue to rely totally on fossil fuels for transportation. Perhaps 'greening' will require that cities are served by local agricultural markets in order to reduce the distance travelled by food, and by waste as it is returned to the land. Perhaps wider use will have to be made of information technology systems, if business continues to be conducted globally, although the need for face-to-face contact must also be recognized. Perhaps it may be necessary for power to be generated and for the associated waste heat to be used locally; or for energy to be gathered from renewable resources at a scale related to the city. Perhaps it may be necessary for industry to make its products by sustainable technologies, for consumption regionally or locally rather than globally. Perhaps – implicit in all these proposals – it may be necessary for cities to be based on the scale of the human, walking and standing rather than driving and sitting.

Such an approach will generate urban spaces which people recognize as relating to them and which they will therefore use. Design details will also change; in place of the simplistic details which need a certain brightness and boldness to be seen by someone moving past at speed it will be possible to return to levels of detail and pattern which were commonplace in earlier days when cities were organized for foot traffic. For the driver or passenger isolated within the protected environment of the car, buildings become virtually contiguous, as people transfer from building to car and car to building. This denial of any external natural environment within the city is as alienating as any closed environment in science fiction.[10] By returning the city to the pedestrian, people are brought into contact with the natural environment. At the very least, such contact may make it harder to ignore the relationship between the natural and the man-made.

Even in the green city the need for transport must be recognized, but such transport must be arranged to create a minimum of thermal or other pollution.

A pedestrian pocket. Land is saved by a greater density of buildings compared to a normal suburb, and walking is encouraged by pathways that connect the whole site without crossing any street

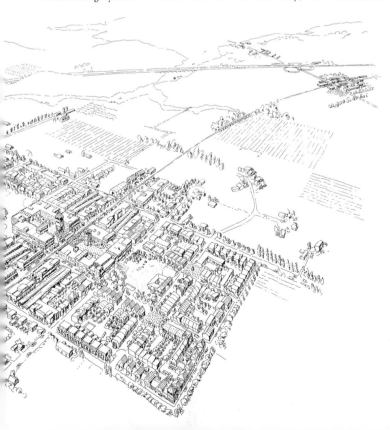

A street for people in Norwich, England; urban design on a pedestrian scale

High rise buildings, Docklands development, London: a cityscape perhaps best viewed at a distance, or from a moving vehicle

FAR RIGHT
The town of Nördingen, Bavaria: a medieval settlement with many of the attributes of the 'pedestrian pocket' proposal

Public transport of the most energy efficient kind, such as tram or rail travel, will need to provide the backbone of the system, Provision must also be made for the passage of essential service vehicles. Solar cars powered from photovoltaic cells could provide for short to medium distance travel, but the size, power and speed of such cars will be very different from the vehicles of today. Because of their low speeds they might mingle with pedestrians, and they would have more in common with the technology of the bicycle than with the supercar of the end of the twentieth century. Even now, it is possible to see a mix of foot, bicycle and vehicular traffic (although still petrol powered) in some residential streets in the Netherlands. The *woonerf* is so organized that through the selection of suitable materials for the hard surfaces, obstructions and planting, cars are forced to go at a speed where they can safely mix with pedestrians or children playing.

By limiting the impact of personal transport on the city it becomes possible to introduce more green spaces, just as in the case of the *woonerf*. Instead of driving through the forests, the city-dweller can have the trees and birds brought into the centre of housing and working areas. Through a change in the scale on which it is based, the green city can encourage an intimacy that has been lost in a society based on fossil energy use. Far from embodying the unified vision of a single human being, the green city will be as individual as each of its closely related parts and occupants requires it to be.

A Dutch *woonerf*, with hard surfaces and planting designed to slow down motor traffic to a speed at which it can safely mix with people, walking or cycling

POSTSCRIPT

Towards a green aesthetic

It has been argued that it is no longer sufficient that the design satisfies the client, can be built within the budget allowed, and earns the aesthetic approval of architectural peers; the designer of a building must also realize the responsibility that resides in making any part of the built environment, however small – that design for the few affects the many.

SOME designers will claim that the whole question of the need for a green architecture is not yet proven. In response it is tempting to point to Pascal's wager,[1] for when proof is finally available that there is no alternative to a green architecture, it will be too late to act. Some may argue that it is already too late, and that change is therefore not worthwhile. In fact, what is being asked of designers is no more than an act of faith, in accepting that greater concern is required for the performance of a building and the materials and methods with which it is made. This does not signify that appearance is unimportant, but allows other issues priority within the design process.

The question of what a green architecture might look like has been touched upon in the preceding chapters. At the present time so few examples of a green approach to the built environment exist that it may be appropriate to glance back to the vernacular architectures that did espouse the green approach for some clues. But it must be recognized that a green architecture does not mean a return to such traditions. In a world of five billion people that is not possible. It is the attitude to materials and resources expressed in the vernacular approach that needs to be accommodated in a future architecture.

In search of a visual identity for the green approach it may be helpful to look at settlements which were designed and planned but were constructed to respect rather than override the environment. Two communities that produced such settlements were the Moravians in Britain and the Shakers in America.

Some seven Moravian settlements were established in Britain and Ireland in the second half of the eighteenth century. They resulted from the desire to build a community that reflected the commitment of those living there to a particular religious belief. Life in the community was uncomplicated and centred on the church. It was recognized that the community had to be fed and money had to be earned, but if the environment was to supply a living for the believers, then the environment had to be respected. The Shakers believed that their settlements should reclaim poor land and improve it as part of their realization of the construction of heaven on earth.

Such an attitude towards the natural world did not mean, however, that it was to remain unaltered. Both the Moravian and Shaker settlements are built in the image of an ideal prototype, but an image that could be modified if necessary. The Moravian settlement of Fairfield in Manchester is closest to the ideal form. The community is centred on the chapel and its burying ground, with the large

The green architecture of the future will be shaped by an approach to site and materials typical of the vernacular traditions. The brick-built Moravian settlement of Ockbrook, Derbyshire, is the architectural expression of a society that believed in human stewardship of the earth

houses for the single brethren and the single sisters set at either side, reflecting the separate seating arrangements within the chapel. Two wide paved streets and a cross street spring from this point to create a central block containing the chapel. Family houses, the schools and other accommodation are grouped along these streets, and through a gateway a narrow road links the community to the Manchester suburb of Droylsden.

Elsewhere Moravian communities could not find land which suited the building of the ideal form centred upon the chapel. On a steep hillside at Fulneck, near Bradford, the community is formed along two parallel streets which run with the contours of the hill. At either end of the main street are gateways and the chapel is placed at the mid-point of the street. The ideal is modified to suit the naturally occurring conditions: the site is

never overridden to meet the intellectual ideal of the community.

The Shakers, too, constructed their communities in accordance with a set of rules that governed their way of life. Although they purchased the poorest land which they reformed and repaired through organic agriculture their need to build heaven on earth resulted in a calm, simple but clear organization of the settlement. Where something of God is recognizable in everyone, heaven could appear in a form evidently of human ordering.

The architecture of the communities, like the vernacular, makes use of the locally available materials: timber in the New England Shaker settlements, brick at Fairfield and stone at Fulneck. The Shakers often constructed their family houses larger than was necessary at the time of building to allow

expansion without inconvenience. In other instances Shaker buildings were altered and enlarged; and materials and elements like doors and windows were re-used. At Fairfield, buildings were altered or replaced over time. Nor did the new buildings merely copy the old; some later houses were taller in proportion, reflecting the concern of the time with the relationship between volumes of fresh air and healthy living.[2] Elsewhere, polychromatic brickwork stands next to the earlier, plain Georgian buildings. Such examples reflect the living nature of the community. It is the difference between an evolutionary approach and the wholesale redevelopment that has disfigured so many communities. Only since the technologies for resource exploitation have been available have designers responded with ideas that sweep away previous developments to

replace them with new 'ideal' solutions that ignore the methods and values established over time.

Such impermanence is justified in terms of 'progress', as if intellectual development were somehow not possible without it, but within the overall framework of respect for resources, much is possible.

Architecture, if it be an art form, is one that is not only reinterpreted by each new set of users but, because of its physical longevity, has to respond to physical changes required by new generations. In the way that the spoken story was once altered as it was handed down, so architecture must be similarly reinterpreted if it is to be useful to succeeding generations, until the point where it has so little relevance that it is demolished, or left to become a ruin. An architecture which is so fixed that, like the written word, it has to be

Timber built Shaker house, the Central Family Dwelling, Shakertown, Kentucky

Double staircase of the Family Dwelling, South Union, Kentucky: elegant forms that express local materials used

RIGHT
Shakertown, Pleasant Hill, Kentucky: the ordered simplicity of a Shaker settlement in its landscape

privately reinterpreted by the individual lacks the dimension of that which can be of use to the whole, changing, community. This is, again, the difference between the Abbé Laugier's approach to the primitive hut which, once built, was complete, and that of Thoreau who only built as much as satisfied immediate needs. Within the second approach, both the Shakers and the Moravians were able to set up a system of architectural design that could be repeated so that it belongs recognizably to them and no others, but which could be altered and readjusted over many years. What is constant to green design is not its appearance, but the way in which it performs, how it provides shelter, comfort and a space to contain the activities required by the users of the time.

Aristotle explained the relationship between soul and body by the following simile:

It is the same as is the case with a house: the rationale will be something like 'A covering preventative of destruction by wind, rain and sun'. But while one philosopher will say that the house is composed of stones, bricks and beams, another will say that it is the form in these things for the given purposes.[3]

Aristotle's argument centres on the idea that a living thing is known, not by what it appears to be but by what it does and the responses it makes to its environment.

You employ stone, wood and concrete, and with these materials you build houses and palaces; that is construction. Ingenuity is at work. But suddenly you touch my heart, you do me good, I am happy and I say: 'This is beautiful.' That is architecture. Art enters in.[4]

Thus Le Corbusier's definition, first quoted at the opening of the discussion, sets forth the order in which architecture is perceived. It is necessary to begin by providing a common ground by which both architect and user perceive the same building. Without such a common ground, a shared value judgement, the heart cannot be touched with beauty. Without the stone, wood and concrete technology, there is no architecture.

To survive on a planet with five billion people requires that a shared system of values is arrived at, so that the ramifications of any action are anticipated, both now and for the future. An architecture that would look at buildings with a similar judgement, and determine beauty through performance might not be so bad. For too long architecture has been dragged into the inaccessibility of fine art, only obtainable by the very rich or in a poor reproduction by those less wealthy. Maybe a green approach to the built environment will succeed not least because it can provide again an architecture for all.

Notes on the text

INTRODUCTION

1 Le Corbusier (1923), trans. as *Towards a new architecture*, F. Etchells, London 1946, p. 187.
2 R. W. Brunskill, *Illustrated Handbook of Vernacular Architecture*, 2nd edn, London 1978, p. 25.
3 J. J. Coulton, *Greek Architects at Work*, 1977 (1982 edn), p. 30.
4 ibid., p. 140.
5 HRH The Prince of Wales, *A Vision of Britain*, London, New York 1989, p. 91.
6 M. Laugier (1753), trans. as *An Essay on Architecture*, Los Angeles 1977, pp. 12–13.
7 H. D. Thoreau (1854), repr. *Walden and Civil Disobedience*, London, New York, 1983, p. 131.
8 Bertolt Brecht, 'Ballade über die frage: "wovon lebt der Mensch?"' from K. Weil and B. Brecht, *Die Dreigroschenoper*.
9 Thoreau, op. cit., p. 90.
10 ibid., p. 91
11 ibid., p. 90
12 Laugier, op. cit., p. 22.
13 G. L. Murcutt in Foreword to P. Drew, *Leaves of Iron: Glenn Murcutt: Pioneer of an Australian architectural form*, The Law Book Company Ltd, North Ryde, New South Wales, 1985.
14 A web in this context is a visual representation of the relationships that exist within an eco-system.
15 Thoreau, op. cit., p. 87.

1 PURPOSE

1 The Luddites were a group of textile workers who smashed the new machinery introduced into the mills at the start of the Industrial Revolution in Britain, when their traditional jobs were threatened by the new technology.
2 G. Boyle and P. Harper, *Radical Technology*, London 1976, p. 230, quoting A. W. Watts, *Nature, Man and Woman*, New York 1958. On the use of needlessly high levels of technology: A. Lovins, *Soft energy paths: towards a durable peace*, Cambridge, Mass., 1977, p. 40.
3 R. Thorne, 'Cast and wrought iron and their uses in architecture', *Teaching Project on the Use of Steel in Architecture*, Unit 1.1, BSC plc, 1990.
4 Empedocles of Acragas in the fifth century BC put forward the theory that all matter in the world was composed of the four elements of earth, water, fire and air. Oversimplifying his thesis, Empedocles saw the 'soul' or animate essence of living beings as having an existence that was proportionate to the mixture of the four elements in the tangible form of the living being, the characteristic behaviour of the living being resulting from this proportionate mixture. The behaviour of body and soul, therefore arose from observable nature.
5 William Morris, 'Prologue: The Wanderers', 'The Earthly Paradise', 1868.
6 G. Howard, 'Modern petrol's power struggle', *Car*, November 1987, and Anon, 'Unleaded – not as green as it seems', *Car*, July 1989.
7 F. Pearce, *Turning up the Heat*, London 1989, pp. 16–17.
8 Department of Environment, *Pollution Paper No. 5*, 'Chlorofluorocarbons and their effect on stratospheric ozone', HMSO, London, 1976.
9 Farman *et al*, *Nature*, vol. 315, 1985, pp. 207–10.
10 Pearce, op. cit., pp. 18–24.
11 S. Boyle and J. Ardill, *The Greenhouse Effect*, London 1989, pp. 81–3.
12 ibid., pp. 33–4.
13 Quoted in ibid., p. 12.
14 R. Brautigan, *Trout Fishing in America*, London 1972, p. 36.
15 S. V. Szokolay, *Environmental Science Handbook*, The Construction Press, London 1980, p. 421.
16 G. Smith, *Economics of Water Collection and Waste Recycling*, Working Paper 6, University of Cambridge, Department of Architecture, Technical Research Division, 1973, and also Yorkshire Water Authority, 1981, private communication.
17 R. Arvill, *Man and Environment*, London 1983, and also C. Kirby, *Water in Great Britain*, London 1984.
18 Szokolay, op. cit., p. 422.
19 ibid.
20 B. and R. Vale, *The Autonomous House*, London 1975, p. 140.
21 Yorkshire Water Authority, 1981, private communication.
22 S. Gordon, *Down the Drain*, London 1989.
23 Yorkshire Water Authority, op. cit.
24 C. Kirby, *Water in Great Britain*, London 1984, p. 112.
25 Holdgate et al, *The World Environment 1972–1982*, Tycooly International, Dublin 1982, quoted in I. G. Simmons, *Changing the Face of the Earth*, Oxford 1989, p. 312.
26 Gordon, op. cit., p. 43.
27 R. Smith, *Air and Rain: the beginnings of a chemical climatology*, 1872.
28 T. N. Skoulikidis, 'Effects of primary and secondary air pollutants and acid depositions on (ancient and modern) buildings and monuments', Paper presented to Symposium on Acid Deposition; A Challenge for Europe, Commission of the European Communities, Karlsruhe, 1983.
29 J. McCormick, *Acid Earth*, Earthscan Publications Ltd, London 1989, p. 187.
30 F. Pearce, 'The strange death of Europe's trees', *New Scientist*, 4 December 1986, pp. 41–5.
31 McCormick, op. cit.
32 D. Hinrichsen, 'Multiple pollutants and forest decline', *Ambio*, 15 May 1986.
33 D. Hinrichsen, 'Acid rain and forest decline' in E. Goldsmith and N. Hilyard (eds.), *The Earth Report: the essential guide to global ecological issues*, Los Angeles 1987.
34 McCormick, op. cit.
35 Ministry of Supply and Services, *Downwind: the acid rain story*, Ottawa, Canada, 1982.
36 T. S. Eliot, *Selected Poems*, London 1954, p. 97.
37 The World Commission on Environment and Development, *Our Common Future* (Brundtland Report), Oxford 1987, p. 192.
38 Watt Committee on Energy, *An assessment of energy resources: Report No. 9*, London 1980.
39 S. Boyle and J. Ardill, op. cit.
40 United Nations, *Population Bulletin of the United Nations No. 14*, New York, 1983.
41 The World Commission on Environment and Development, op. cit., p. 96.
42 ibid., pp. 169–70.
43 G. Leach *et al*, *A Low-energy Strategy for the UK*, International Institute for Environment and Development (IIED), 1979.
44 D. Olivier, H. Miall *et al*, *Energy efficient futures: opening the solar option*, Earth Resources Research, London 1983.
45 Department of Energy, *Renewable energy in the U.K.: the way forward*, Energy Paper No. 55, HMSO, London 1988.
46 Building Research Establishment, 'Energy conservation: a study of energy in housing', *BRE Current Paper CP56/75*, BRE, 1975.
47 Italo Calvino, *Invisible Cities*, London 1979, p. 66.
48 Sant'Elia, *Messagio* (1914), quoted in Reyner Banham, *Theory and Design in the First Machine Age*, London 1960, p. 129.
49 I. G. Simmons, *Changing the Face of the Earth*, Oxford 1989, pp. 236–7.
50 G. Moss, *Britain's Wasting Acres*, London 1981, p. 73.
51 Szokolay, op. cit., p. 421.
52 ibid.
53 CIBS Building Energy Code, Part 4; these target values for use in the design of different building types are those classified as 'good' in performance. They are issued by The Chartered

Institute of Building Services Engineers, London: *Measurement of energy consumption and comparison with targets for existing buildings*, CIBS, London 1982.

54 Self-build houses at the Findhorn Foundation are designed by Keystone Architects and Designers Cooperative. The first two were built by members with three weeks' instructive supervision by Constructive Individuals.

2 PERFORMANCE

1 B. Ward, *The Home of Man*, London 1976, p. 280.

2 F. Kafka (1916), 'Metamorphosis', in *Metamorphosis and other stories*, repr. London 1965, p. 26.

3 Reyner Banham, *The Architecture of the Well-Tempered Environment*, London 1969, pp. 182–3.

4 Kafka, 'Metamorphosis', op. cit., p. 27.

5 H. Kyrk, *Economic Problems of the Family*, New York 1933, p. 99, quoted in Adrian Forty, *Objects of Desire*, London 1986, p. 211.

6 J. S. Norgard, 'Improved efficiency in domestic electricity use', *Energy Policy*, No. 7, March 1979, pp. 43–56, quoted in D. Olivier, H. Miall, et al, op. cit., p. 78.

7 L. Shorrock, 'The Greenhouse Effect', *Building Services: the CIBSE Journal*, July 1989, p. 65.

8 In the summer of 1989, the UK Government responded to the problem of global warming by suggesting an increased programme of nuclear power. In November 1989, however, nuclear stations were withdrawn from the privatization sale of the electricity industry, on the grounds that they were too expensive to operate. At the time, no alternative strategy for power production to reduce carbon dioxide was proposed.

9 The Watt Committee on Energy, *Assessment of Energy Resources*, Report No. 9, The Watt Committee on Energy Ltd, London 1981, p. 55.

10 S. Boyle and J. Ardill, *The Greenhouse Effect*, London 1989.

11 C. C. Swan, 'Light-powered architecture', *Architectural Record*, March 1988, p. 126.

12 Kafka, 'Metamorphosis', op. cit., p. 50.

13 The World Commission on Environment and Development, *Our Common Future*, Oxford 1987, p. 34.

14 The table gives values for 1975 from South Yorkshire County Council, *Refuse Incineration Plant, Bernard Road, Sheffield*.

15 B. and R. Vale, *The Self-sufficient House*, London 1980, pp. 113–14.

16 A. Ortega, W. Rybczynski, S. Ayad, W. Ali, A. Acheson, *The Ecol Operation*, Minimum Cost Housing Group, School of Architecture, McGill University, Montreal, Canada, 1972, p. 20.

17 F. Wilson, 'Cleansing the Land We Build Upon', *Architecture*, August 1989, p. 99.

18 M. Pawley, *Garbage Housing*, London 1975, p. 23.

19 ibid., p. 34.

20 B. Voyd in P. Oliver, *Shelter and Society*, London 1969, p. 156 (1976 ed.).

21 Kafka, 'Metamorphosis', op. cit., p. 21.

22 The World Commission on Environment and Development, *Our Common Future*, Oxford 1987, p. 16.

23 S. Lawson, 'Agricultural Policy and Technical Change' in *Agricultural Policy for the UK*, Technology Policy Group, Occasional Paper 1, Open University 1980, p. 5.

24 In the ten years during which the authors lived on a 0.75 Ha small-holding with a family of three small children, they grew 75 per cent of the value of their food for an expenditure of time that averaged 2 hours per day. Self-sufficiency on an annual basis was achieved in milk, butter, fats, meat, eggs, fruit, vegetables and honey. See also R. Vale, 'Towards a new agriculture' in *Agricultural Policy for the UK*, Technology Policy Group, Occasional Paper 1, Open University, Milton Keynes, 1980.
In the USA in 1990 the population density was 25 persons per square kilometre; in Britain, 230 persons per square kilometre. There was some ten acres of land per person in the USA, and just over one acre of land per person in Britain.

25 G. Leach, *Energy and Food Production*, International Institute for Environment and Development, London 1975.

26 Franz Kafka, 'Metamorphosis', op. cit., p. 7.

27 In 1990 in the UK, cars put some 3,000 tons of lead annually into the atmosphere. This heavy metal accumulates in the body and damages the brains of children, including the unborn. After the pricing of fuel in the UK to make unleaded petrol cheaper, some 25 per cent of cars used unleaded fuel.

28 In Britain, for example, only about half of the population held a licence to drive a car in 1990.

29 P. Steadman, *Energy, Environment and Building*, Cambridge, 1975, p. 286.

30 C. Williams-Ellis (ed.), *Britain and the Beast*, London 1938.

3 PRACTICE

PRINCIPLE 1: CONSERVATION

1 G. M. Davies, N. S. Sturrock and A. C. Benson, 'Some results of measurements on St George's School, Wallasey', *Journal of the Institution of Heating and Ventilating Engineers*, July, Vol. 13, 1971, pp. 77–84.

2 *SCALA 1989 Yearbook*, pp. 43–6, Reed Information Services Ltd, East Grinstead, 1989.

3 The R-2000 programme has been sponsored by the Canadian Federal Department of Energy, Mines and Resources and the Canadian Home Builders' Association. The 'R' stands for 'Resistance' (to heat loss) and the 2000 suggests that the houses are designed for the year 2000 and beyond.

4 Commission of the European Communities, 'Low Energy House G, Hjortekaer, Denmark', *Project Monitor*, Issue 41, February 1989. School of Architecture, University College, Dublin.

5 Commission of the European Communities, 'Lou Souleu; Avignon, France', *Project Monitor*, Issue 20, April 1988. School of Architecture, University College, Dublin.

6 S. V. Szokolay, *World Solar Architecture*, London 1980, pp. 94–5.

7 S. Ashley, 'What the Doctor Ordered', *Building Services: the CIBSE Journal*, April 1988.

8 Commission of the European Communities, 'Casa Termicamente Optimizada, Porto, Portugal', *Project Monitor*, Issue 9, December 1987. School of Architecture, University College, Dublin.

PRINCIPLE 2: DESIGNING WITH NATURE

1 K. Butti and J. Perlin, *A Golden Thread*, Cheshire Books, Palo Alto, California, 1980.

2 ibid.

3 P. Buchanan, 'Guest House for Missionaries; Dar-es-Salaam', *Architectural Review*, August 1985, pp. 62–5.

4 P. Drew, *Leaves of Iron: Glenn Murcutt: Pioneer of an Australian architectural form*, The Law Book Company, North Ride, New South Wales, 1985.

5 S. V. Szokolay, *World Solar Architecture*, London 1980.

6 Commission of the European Communities, 'Istituto Tecnico Commerciale; Montefiascone, Italy', *Project Monitor*, Issue 38, February 1989. School of Architecture, University College, Dublin.

7 Commission of the European Communities, 'Ecole primaire de Tournai; Tournai, Belgium', *Project Monitor*, Issue 18, April 1988. School of Architecture, University College, Dublin.

8 Commission of the European Communities, 'Les Gárennes; Saint-Quentin-en-Yvelines, France', *Project Monitor*, Issue 36, February 1989. School of Architecture, University College, Dublin.

9 Commission of the European Communities, 'Orbassano; Torino, Italy', *Project Monitor*, Issue

26, July 1988. School of Architecture, University College, Dublin.

10 G. Darley, 'Hampshire symbol', *Architectural Review*, No. 1072, 1986.

11 F. Duffy 'SAS Co-operation', *Architectural Review*, No. 1105, March 1989.

PRINCIPLE 3: MINIMIZING NEW RESOURCES

1 For example, upon construction of the Victoria and Albert Museum in London, the Brompton Boilers building was no longer required, and in 1865 the iron building was offered to the authorities of North, South and East London with the intention that it should be re-erected as a local museum. East London accepted it, and the building opened as the Bethnal Green Museum in 1872. It is today the Museum of Childhood.

2 The Internationale Bauausstellung (IBA) was formed to regenerate West Berlin in areas which had been destroyed or heavily damaged by the war. The Neubau section of IBA concentrated on new build, while the Altbau section was to regenerate areas that were seriously damaged but still occupied by thriving, if poor, communities. Following the winding up of IBA in 1987, Altbau has been reformed as STERN (Gesellschaft der behutsamen Stadterneuerung Berlin) to continue the work of urban renewal.

3 P. Davey, 'STERN Work', *Architectural Review*, April, 1987, pp. 86–9.

4 E. M. Farelly, 'Renting on the Riverfront: Brandram's Housing Co-op', *The Architects' Journal*, 3 February 1988, pp. 29–42.

5 P. Buchanan, 'The nostalgic now', *Architectural Review*, January 1988, p. 65.

6 C. Slessor, 'Construction Study', *The Architects' Journal*, 9 December 1987, p 55.

7 B. Helliwell and N. McNamara, 'Hand-built Houses of Hornby Island', *Architectural Design*, July 1978, p. 478.

8 H. Hertzberger, 'Architect's Account', *The Architects' Journal*, 29 October 1975.

9 Commission of the European Communities, 'Baggesensgade; Copenhagen, Denmark', *Project Monitor*, Issue 17, April. School of Architecture, University College, Dublin.

PRINCIPLE 4: RESPECT FOR USERS

1 P. Blundell-Jones, 'Woodland Retreat', *The Architects' Journal*, 27 September 1989, p. 28.

2 The community action group took the name 'the Eldonians' from Eldon Street, which contained the Church of Our Lady of Reconciliation.

3 R. Cowan, P. Hannay and R. Owens, 'The light on top of the tunnel', *The Architects' Journal*, 23 March 1988, pp. 37–63.

4 ibid., p. 49.

5 P. Blundell-Jones, 'Graz', *The Architects' Review*, December 1988, p. 81.

6 L. Kroll, *The Architecture of Complexity*, London 1986.

7 C. Alexander *et al*, *The Production of Houses*, Oxford 1985, p. 63.

8 R. Spence, 'Grass-roots Tech', *The Architectural Review*, July 1987, p. 59.

PRINCIPLE 5: RESPECT FOR SITE

1 G. L. Murcutt in Foreword to P. Drew, *Leaves of Iron: Glenn Murcutt: Pioneer of an Australian architectural form*, The Law Book Company Ltd, North Ryde, New South Wales, 1985.

2 T. Faegre, *Tents: architecture of the nomads*, London 1979.

3 P. Buchanan, 'Barely there', *Architectural Review*, No. 1087, 1987.

4 D. A. Oppenheimer, 'Prefabricated house perches lightly on a sloping site', *Architecture*, July 1985.

5 L. Weaver, *The 'Country Life' book of cottages costing from £150 to £600*, Country Life Ltd, London 1913.

6 B. Rudofsky, *Architecture without architects*, The Museum of Modern Art, New York, 1965.

7 L. Gropp, *Solar Houses*, New York 1978.

8 Commission of the European Communities, 'Llavaneres semi-buried house, Catalunya, Spain'. *Project Monitor*, Issue 37, February 1989. School of Architecture, University College, Dublin.

9 Erisco/Bauder Ltd, *Erisco-Bauder Green Roof Systems*, Erisco/Bauder Ltd, Ipswich, Suffolk, 1989.

10 Redland Roof Tiles Ltd, *The Redland Roofing Manual 1988*, Redland Roof Tiles Limited, Reigate, Surrey.

11 Commission of the European Communities, 'Solarhaus Issum, Issum, Germany', *Project Monitor*, Issue 40, February 1989. School of Architecture, University College, Dublin.

PRINCIPLE 6: HOLISM

1 N. Edwards, 'Introducing the thick building', *Building Services: The CIBSE Journal*, January 1990.

2 F. Duffy, 'The European Challenge', *The Architects' Journal*, 17 August 1988. W. Holdsworth, 'Organic services', *Building Services: The CIBSE Journal*, March 1989.

4   PROPOSAL: GROUND RULES FOR THE GREEN CITY

1 Le Corbusier, *The City of Tomorrow*, trans. F. Etchells, London 1929, p. 192.

2 Land was to be redistributed by the State so that each childless couple would have a minimum of one acre, and larger families more: see Frank Lloyd Wright, 'Broadacre City', *The Architectural Record*, LXXCII, April 1935.

3 ibid.

4 G. H. Gray, *Housing and Citizenship*, New York 1946, p. 97.

5 D. Stamp, *The Land of Britain, its use and misuse*, London 1948. R. H. Best and J. T. Ward, 'The Garden Controversy', *Studies in Rural Land Use, Report No. 2*, Wye College, University of London, 1956.

6 D. Kelbaugh (ed.), *The Pedestrian Pocket Book: a new suburban design strategy*, Princeton Architectural Press, 1989.

7 D. Walker, *The architecture and planning of Milton Keynes*, Architectural Press, London 1982.

8 L. Thomas, 'Can a suburb be like a small town?, *US News and World Report*, 5 March 1990.

9 J. McCloud, 'Homes planned a walk from shops and jobs', *The New York Times*, 4 March 1990.

10 For example the novelist E. M. Forster, 'The Machine Stops' in *Collected Short Stories*, 1947.

POSTSCRIPT

1 Pascal proposed that the sensible course was to believe in God, for if God exists then Heaven is attained through belief, and if God does not exist, then nothing will have been lost by believing in Him. If one chose not to believe in God and he does exist, then oneself is the loser. If one chooses not to believe in the necessity of a green approach to architecture, and the green approach is later shown to be the only viable option, the loss is not confined to the individual. The architectural profession owes it to the peoples of the world to take up the Green Wager.

2 The Victorian belief that fresh air was essential for the prevention of disease led to building laws that stipulated high ceilings and permanent open ventilators (usually in the form of air bricks) in rooms.

3 Aristotle, *De Anima*, trans. H. Lawson-Tancred, London 1986, p. 129.

4 Le Corbusier (1923), *Towards a new architecture*, trans. F. Etchells, London 1946, p. 187.

Acknowledgments

The authors would like to offer grateful thanks to all the architects, designers and photographers who so willingly offered material for inclusion in this book. Information sources are acknowledged in the Notes on the text, illustration sources are listed below. Page number are followed by top (t), bottom (b), centre (c), left (l), right (r).

Agence Française pour la Maîtrise de l'Energie 80b; Air Pollution Control District, County of LA 16–17; ANP Foto, Amsterdam 67, 180; Arcaid/photo © Richard Bryant 11b; Carlos Araújo & Santiago Boissel 83b, 84t; James Austin 108; F. Javier Barba: front cover right (photo Lluis Casals), 137, 146–7; Hans Bertram, Munich 179; Peter Blundell Jones 120; BMW (GB) Ltd 66cr, 66b; Lucien Bouat, Yves Draussin, Jean Massip/Photographies Jean Biaugeaud & Cie 92–3, 101b, 102; Bournville P. R. Services 172–3t; Branson Coates Architecture Ltd/ photo © Eddie Valentine-Hames 112; Courtesy British Gas 51t; Building Research Establishment, Crown Copyright 46–7; Calthorpe Associates 176b, 177; Canadian Homebuilders Association 76tr; Centraal Beheer, Apeldoorn 125, 126, back cover, below right; CEGB National Power Division 52; Centre For Alternative Technology/photo Jean Welstead, Machynlleth 136b; Ross Chapple 35, 138; David Clarke Associates 39b, 121, 172–3b; Don Corner 136tr; Danfoss Ltd 51b; Billy Davis, III Aerial Photography, Inc., Anchorage, Kentucky 184–5; The ECD Partnership 89t, 96, 99, 104l; Eldonian Development Trust 130; Courtesy of The Electricity

Association 73; Energy Advisory Associates, Milton Keynes 77t; The Environmental Picture Library/ photo © Susan I. Cunningham 31; Erisco-Bauder Ltd 140; Ford Motor Company Ltd 16; Michael Freeman 183, 184; French Government Tourist Office 64b; Roberto Gabetti & Aimaro Isola 104r; General Motors Europe 66t; A.H. Heineken 61t; Bo Helliwell, Blue Sky Archive 122; Hubert-Jan Henket 84–5; Prof. Thomas Herzog 128; Hirmer Verlag 10–11t; Howden Wind Turbines Ltd 53, back cover left; Eilfried Huth 118–19, 131, 132–3; The ICCE Photo Library 26; Installa Energietechnik, Issum 149; IPR scrl, Viterbo 89b; Ray Kennedy 182; Stefan Koppelkamm 110; Lucien Kroll 116–17, 134–5; Kvaerner a.s., Oslo 30; Levitt Bernstein Associates Ltd 111, 113; London Docklands Development Corporation 178b; Joe Low, Southampton 105; Manchester City Council 22; Masters Corporation, front cover below left, 114–15; William McDonough Architects 41, 129 (Brenda King); McGill University 60; Klaus Meier-Ude 64–5; Metcalf and Associates 55t (Maxwell Mackenzie), 93r; Metrocentre Marketing Department 27; Glenn Murcutt 36b, 88b; Glenn Murcutt/photo © Max Dupain 2, 86–7; Photography courtesy, The Museum of Modern Art, New York 49; NASA 54b; NMB Postbank Group 157b (Sybolt Voeten), 158–9 (Jan Derwig), 158–9 insets (Sybolt Voeten), 160 (Jan Derwig), 162–3 (Bob Fleumer), 165 (Jan van der Weerd); Norfolk County Council Library and Information Service 178t; Robin Parow 98; Martin Pawley 60–1; Robert Perron 6, 33, 34t, 145; Rosmarie Pierer 17; Gabriel

Poole 142; © photo RMN, Paris 109; RIBA, London 174–5b; Rocky Mountain Institute 34b, 74–5; SAS, Stockholm 94–5, 95–r (Ewa Rudling), 106, 107 (Ewa Rudling), back cover top right (Ewa Rudling) right; Scandia-Hus Ltd. 50t; Science Photo Library 36t (Robin Scagell), 37 (Peter Menzel); John Simpson & Partners/Painting by Carl Laubin 10b; Solarex 38t; M. G. Souvatzides 40; St George's School, Wallasey 70–1; Floyd Kenneth Stein 127; Stramit Industries Ltd 58–9; Sunergy. Distribution by Multiple Connections Ltd 54t, 55bl; Dr Steven V. Szokolay 81t; A. Tombazis 38–9; Bertel Udsen 77b, 78–9; Brenda and Robert Vale 82, 150–2, 157t; Vattenfall Elteknik AB 45b; Volvo 66cl; Water Pollution Research Laboratory, Crown Copyright reserved 25; Weimar Archive, GB 172; Malcolm Wells 19, 139, 144; Jean Wilfart 90–1, 100–1t, front cover, top left; Wotan Lamps Ltd 45t; Frank Lloyd Wright Memorial Foundation 171; Yorkshire Brick Company 56.

In addition to those above, the following introductory, uncaptioned illustrations are gratefully acknowledge: p. 15: section of head of wind turbine Modern Power Systems, London; p. 43: diagram of solar roof panel and heat exchange ventilation, Ecole Primaire de Tournai, Belgium; p. 69: section drawing of underground house, reproduced with permission from *An architect's sketchbook of Underground Buildings: Drawings and Photographs*, published by Malcolm Wells, 673 Satucket Road, Brewster, Massachusetts; p. 169: high-density housing, reproduced by permission Calthorpe Associates.

Index